Praise for Jim Hardy and
The Plane Truth for Golfers

"Jim Hardy is the most knowledgeable teacher in golf. I say this based on my association with Jim as my friend and golf instructor for nearly 20 years. No other instructor has his understanding of golf swing techniques and what makes them work. I met Jim at Riviera Country Club during the 1983 PGA championship. It was early in the week and I was hitting the ball poorly. I asked Jim for help, and by the week's end, on a Sunday afternoon, I was standing on the 72nd hole of a major championship tied for the lead. Although I did not win, that week was the beginning of a great journey with this remarkable man. Any golfer, regardless of ability, who has the opportunity to listen and work with Jim will benefit and improve."

—Peter Jacobsen, winner of seven PGA Tour championships and 2004 U.S. Senior Open

"I was a top 30 PGA Tour player, and like all golfers I wanted to get better. That effort turned into a nightmare. Within two years, I had practically fallen off the Tour. At my lowest point, I was recommended to Jim Hardy. He convinced me that the instruction I had been pursuing did not match my swing type. I abandoned the harmful instruction and learned what worked for me. Thanks to Jim, since that turn around, I have become a multiple tournament winner."

—Scott McCarron, winner of three PGA Tour championships

"All my life I have been a great admirer of Ben Hogan and built my swing around his principles. My career had been a constant struggle between success and failure. By the time I met Jim Hardy, the failure was far outweighing the success. Jim explained why my swing was failing. I understood for the first time that there are two sets of fundamentals. We simply eliminated the ones that did not belong in my swing, and within six months I had won a PGA Tour title and 1.4 million dollars."

—Tom Pernice, Jr., winner of two PGA Tour championships

"I've been working with Jim Hardy for about 10 years. Every time I get into a slump, and they are now far and few between, I go visit Jim and he always knows what swing part I've got wrong and fixes it. What's amazing is how quickly I get results. I also like the fact that he's never really changed my swing. Instead, he taught me what works in my swing and what does not. Jim's the greatest, and I'm so pleased that he is sharing his secrets with golfers in *The Plane Truth for Golfers*."
— Duffy Waldorf, winner of four PGA Tour championships

"Jim Hardy is the best communicator I have ever heard on the lesson tee, and I believe he is about to be recognized as one of the top three or four instructors in golf. He is that good."
— Jim Achenbach, *Golfweek* magazine senior writer and former winner of the World Golf Writers' Championship

"Finally, there's a book that clarifies the fundamentals of golf based on a swing-shape that is right for you. Hardy has the best golf mind I've ever been around. He has made golf easier to teach and learn. You know exactly what to work on and what to avoid. I have seen it with my own eyes. Using his approach, my students improve at a faster rate. Their swing-throughs are simpler, so they can get beyond swing mechanics and get on with playing the game. They are hitting longer and straighter shots even under pressure. The results are amazing and fast. Read this book and have fun playing golf your way."
— Mike LaBauve, voted by *Golf* and *Golf Digest* magazines as one of America's top teachers

"Jim Hardy has one of the most creative minds in golf. He has studied all the great strikers of the ball to determine the common traits. Not satisfied with his findings, he tossed all the common denominators into a shag bag, shook it gently, and came up with his unique understanding of the one-plane and two-plane golf swings. It does not matter if you have played for years or are just starting the game. You will improve immediately and understand why."
— Shelby Futch, owner and president of Golf Digest Golf Schools and John Jacobs' Golf Schools

The Plane Truth for

Golfers

**Breaking Down the One-Plane Swing
and the Two-Plane Swing and Finding
the One That's Right for You**

Jim Hardy

with

John Andrisani

McGraw-Hill

New York   Chicago   San Francisco   Lisbon   London   Madrid   Mexico City
Milan   New Delhi   San Juan   Seoul   Singapore   Sydney   Toronto

Library of Congress Cataloging-in-Publication Data

Hardy, Jim.
    The plane truth for golfers : breaking down the one-plane swing and the two-plane swing and finding the one that's right for you / by Jim Hardy with John Andrisani.—1st ed.
        p.   cm.
    ISBN 0-07-143245-0
      1. Swing (Golf)—Handbooks, manuals, etc.   I. Andrisani, John.   II. Title.
    GV979.S9H29   2005
    796.352'3—dc22   2004025047

3 4 5 6 7 8 9 10 11 12 13   DOC/DOC 0 9 8 7 6 5

ISBN 0-07-143245-0

Interior photographs by Yasuhiro Tanabe/Beyondship, Inc.

McGraw-Hill books are available at special quantity discounts to use as premiums and sales promotions, or for use in corporate training programs. For more information, please write to the Director of Special Sales, Professional Publishing, McGraw-Hill, Two Penn Plaza, New York, NY 10121-2298. Or contact your local bookstore.

This book is printed on acid-free paper.

I dedicate this book to Peter Jacobsen, the driving force behind The Plane Truth for Golfers; *to my daughter, Rachel, and wife, Marilyn, whose love is a daily inspiration to me; and to Him in His Matchless Grace.*

Contents

1   The Choice Is Yours   1

Why you should commit to improving your technique and the

critical factors for determining whether you are a one-plane or

two-plane swinger

2   Getting Set   11

The fundamentals that govern golf's starting position for your

specific type of swing

Foreword

I am so excited that you chose to read *The Plane Truth for Golfers*. Getting this book into your hands has been a goal of mine for about five years. I still haven't figured out if my desire to get Jim Hardy to write this book was a selfish act or a noble gesture. Is it that I wanted my own "bible" of instruction, or did I want every golfer to have this knowledge? To be honest, I think it's both.

Jim Hardy is the most knowledgeable golf-swing scholar you've never heard of in the game of golf today. I say that with confidence because I've worked with all the ones you have heard of. Jim Hardy is an intensely serious person who is passionate about every aspect of his life. Yet, he is one of the most engaging and personable men I've ever met. A self-promoter he is not. I jokingly refer to Jim as a "filet mignon" who's fairly tough on the outside but very soft and rare on the inside.

I lost most of my desire to play competitive golf following my father's death in 1992. I had a brief stint in the booth with Brent Musberger at ABC-TV in 1993, which rekindled my desire to play tournament golf. It was Jim's understanding, advice, and mentoring that helped me get through that difficult time and return to the PGA Tour. Jim's belief in me continues to inspire me today. I wouldn't be the player I am if it weren't for Jim Hardy.

In 1993, I decided to change my swing from a two-plane to a one-plane golf action. I knew that it was going to take a lot of work and patience to pull it off, but I felt that, with Jim's knowledge, I could succeed. *The Plane Truth for Golfers* will explain exactly what a one-plane golf swing is as opposed to a two-plane swing; why they are different, and why you can't mix the distinct fundamentals that serve both methods. This book is your roadmap to understanding *your swing* and improving your golf scores.

When I met Jim in 1983, I had an athletic, homemade action taught to me and my entire family by my father Erling. My dad was a very good player his entire life and even at the time of his death, at the age of 75, was a single-digit handicapper. He did the best he could with us all, but over time, I developed a backswing that started with a dramatic left arm lift, that put the clubhead closed and laid off at the top. My downswing was even more adventuresome, as I started with a hard slide of my hips to the left, swung the club way out to the right, and hit push blocks with a low trajectory and very little backspin. To make things worse, I started to have a lot of back pain—at 29 years of age! I knew I needed some help.

Jim and I started working on my swing and, because I was a two-plane swinger at that time, he gave me an understanding of the fundamentals for that swing. He impressed me with his fresh new theories of his one- and two-plane swings. I vividly remember the 1985 PGA Championship at the Riviera Country Club, as Jim and I worked to get my club more on plane. He had suggested a new position at the top for me to try. I proceeded to do exactly what Jim wanted and hit the biggest block, banana slice about 75 yards to the right, into the middle of the tenth fairway. Needless to say, Jim was excited that I had performed this new on-plane position perfectly, but also suggested that the day before a major championship probably wouldn't be the best time or place to introduce this new move. I proceeded to hit eight or ten more shots close to the same spot in the tenth fairway. As the spectators started to whisper and point, I pronounced myself ready to go into battle with my newly improved swing. Jim wanted to crawl into the deepest divot he could find, thinking he had just taken me out of any chance I had to play well that week. Nevertheless, I was confident that what Jim had told me about the two different types of swings was correct and that now was as good a time as any to throw this new thinking into the line up. Even though it felt different, I believed I had the ability to get it right. So, I went with it all week, hit my share of foul balls, yet stood on the seventy-second tee tied for the lead with eventual champion Hal Sutton and runner-up Jack Nicklaus. The fact that I chickened out on that 18th hole tee shot and bogeyed had nothing to do with Jim at all. I'll take the blame for that one.

Having spent 1983 to 1992 as a two-plane swinger, Jim was always very helpful in explaining to me his theories about his one-plane versus two-plane methods. I was a two-planer but was very curious about the one-plane action. After listening and learning, I knew I wanted to become a one-planer. We both felt I possessed the strength and flexibility to make that change. So, in 1993, we embarked on the experiment of turning a two-plane swinger into a one-planer. And, while I've never had any Nicklaus-like brilliance, I did win twice in 1995. I won again in 2003 at the age of 49, and last summer, at 50, I won the U.S. Senior Open Championship. Although I feel that I still have plenty of work left to do to my swing, Jim has deemed the experiment a success. I've gone from Dr. Jekyll to Mr. Hyde, so to speak.

You'll see that I have done the swing sequence for both the one-plane and two-plane swings. I believe that I'm genuinely qualified since I spent my early PGA Tour years swinging one way and my later years swinging the other. More importantly, you will learn a lot about golf-swing technique by viewing these wonderful photographs. You'll also learn a lot about the one- and two-plane swings by reading about "feelings" that a few of Jim's PGA Tour students have expressed during many of their sessions. I encouraged Jim to include these because they will be helpful as you make corrections and changes to your own swing.

When I was a two-planer, my absolute bedrock fundamentals were a smooth one-two tempo with a dramatic pause at the top. I never rushed or hurried my swing, and I never tried to hit the ball hard. As a one-plane swinger, my thoughts are to rotate my arms around my body as much as possible, literally throwing my arms behind me to the right in my backswing and then turning my body so my arms are thrown through the ball and behind me to the left. I feel like Mark McGwire must feel when he hits one out of the park. I simply rotate my body like a maniac, and I release the club like a baseball player. In short, I feel reckless and I swing hard, but I'm in full control of the golf club.

I pulled Jim back into teaching because his theories are profound. He talks about the golf swing in a way I've never heard before. Before I met Jim, I believed, as the majority of golfers do, that there was one set of fundamentals in the swing, and they applied to everyone. I now know that this is incorrect. I prodded him back into teaching because I wanted him to share his knowledge with some of my friends on the Tour. *The Plane Truth for Golfers* is the result of my pushing him further to share his knowledge with all golfers. There is a tremendous amount of confusion in the teaching of golf today, and it exists on all levels. I've seen some of the most exciting, proficient, and successful Tour players all of a sudden stop hitting fairways and greens. It kills me to see players like Seve Ballesteros, Ian Baker Finch, Bobby Clampett, and Chip Beck struggle with their games to the point of no return. They got confused, as we all do from time to time, yet had no roadmap to get back to where they played their best. Let's hope that those days are over.

It was my concern for some of my close friends on Tour and the state of their games that prompted me to send them to Jim. Scott McCarron, Tom Pernice, Jr., Paul Azinger, Casey Martin, Jay Delsing, Brad Faxon, Olin Browne, and Brian Henninger are some of the players that have worked with Jim and have benefited greatly from his advice. I knew Jim could help them, and he did. Just as I know he can help you. Jim doesn't hang out a shingle as a teacher, and you don't see him as a regular on The Golf Channel. So, *The Plane Truth for Golfers* is your opportunity to take a lesson from him.

I sincerely hope you enjoy this very enlightening and important piece of work. I personally think this extraordinary book will be the most revolutionary instructional book since Ben Hogan's *Five Lessons: The Modern Fundamentals of Golf*. Study hard, learn well, have fun, and good luck.

—Peter Jacobsen

Acknowledgments

I thank my agent Scott Waxman and also editor Mark Weinstein of McGraw-Hill for trusting my new theories on the golf swing enough to publish *The Plane Truth for Golfers*, a book I truly believe will revolutionize the way the game is taught and allow players of varying handicaps to improve.

I also owe credit to all my PGA Tour students, most notably Peter Jacobsen, Tom Pernice, Jr., Scott McCarron, and Duffy Waldorf, who have been with me the longest, as well as the other pro and amateur golfers I've given lessons to over the years. I've learned so much from each and every one of them.

When it comes to those people I'm grateful to for relaying the instructional message, John Andrisani, my co-author, and photographer Yasuhiro Tanabe are at the top of my list. John is the former senior editor of instruction at *Golf* magazine, and Yasuhiro is an experienced photojournalist whose work appears regularly in major golf publications. I also thank Doug Hoxeng, Ph.D., for his editing comments. I owe gratitude as well to both BlackHorse Golf Club in Cypress, Texas, and Windermere Golf Club in Windermere, Florida, for hosting the photography "shoots" for this new book.

I would be remiss to leave out a few other individuals who have mentored me, contributed to my knowledge of the golf swing, and supported my efforts to continue conducting research and collecting data until I discovered the missing links to improvement—there is not one set of fundamentals, but two sets of fundamentals that govern all golf swings. Among them are: Harold Hoffman, my first instructor and second father; John Jacobs, whose genius enlightened and inspired me; LPGA Hall of Fame member Carol Mann, my loyal and wonderful friend; Shelby Futch, my college roommate, co-seeker of golf's mysteries, and lifelong pal; and Labron Harris, Sr., my college golf coach at Oklahoma State University.

Finally, there are a number of fellow golf professionals who have been with me from the beginning in my search for clarity and better understanding of swing technique. Their support, encouragement, and contributions have been great. Thanks to Mike LaBauve, Roger Gunn, Brad Bell, Hank Haney, Jim Murphy, and Mark Miller.

Introduction

I started playing golf when I was 15 years old. I wanted to become the greatest golfer in the world. That didn't happen. What did happen, however, is the most wonderful life in golf that I could ever have imagined. I attended college on a golf scholarship, made All-American, and ended up playing the PGA Tour from 1968–1973. I've been a club professional, a teacher, lecturer, television color commentator, writer, and golf course owner. I built a golf management company and a development company. I've been a partner in a golf course design firm for more than a dozen years with one of the greatest people in the world, Peter Jacobsen. I've traveled the world and played on nearly every golf course of note. I grew up on one of the best, Prairie Dunes Country Club in Hutchinson, Kansas. I've met thousands of terrific people, but if it weren't for my first instructor, Harold Hoffman, the golf professional at Carey Park Golf Course in Hutchinson, none of this would have happened. He was a true pied piper. Kids flocked to him and he in turn loved every one of them. He instilled in all of us a great sense of adventure about golf. It's lasted my lifetime. I have been fortunate to pursue so many avenues in golf, but I'm not sure I'm identified by any one of them. Mostly in golf I've been a learner. I'm an inveterate tinkerer and am happiest when puzzled and trying to find an answer. Everything about golf has always been a challenge to me, a great and wonderful riddle wanting to be solved. It's been that pursuit that has been my lifeblood.

Upon leaving the Tour, I was very fortunate to land a job at a fine old club in the Chicago area, Exmoor Country Club. While at Exmoor, I learned that I didn't know how to teach, and teaching was about the only thing I truly liked about being a club professional. As a player I had gone to a number of teachers and it seemed that each one of them told me something different. I couldn't believe that I had so many different things wrong with my swing. If I did have that many faults, how could I play as well as I did? I knew that one of those teachers was probably right, but which one? I decided to find out. I took speed-reading courses in order to read more instruction books. I telephoned top golf teachers across the country and asked each one if I could visit and watch them coach. I got very confused. Then all of a sudden I got a lot better, thanks to meeting noted instructor John Jacobs from England.

John was so far in front of everything and everyone else it was unbelievable. He understood golf, totally and logically. He was the first to really understand ball flight, how it related to impact conditions, and what the club was doing to cause the impact. He also understood why the club was being swung in the wrong fashion and, most importantly, how to fix it. A lot of mysteries were solved. I began an association with this incredible teacher and ended up co-founding the John Jacobs Golf Schools with my dear friend Shelby Futch. I retired from the golf schools after a few years, and Shelby has since taken them to the number one spot. But back to John Jacobs.

John has a fabulous saying that I agree wholeheartedly with, and it goes something like this: "The sole purpose of the golf swing is to produce a correct, repetitive impact, and the method employed is of no significance as long as it is repetitive."

Our purpose in swinging a golf club cannot be summed up more succinctly. The method that John personally employed and taught was what he would often describe as swinging your arms up and down on the inside as you turn your body—two turns and a swish. The arms swinging up and down while the body turned were done on two separate planes. The body would turn on a somewhat horizontal plane, revolving around a fairly erect spine angle. The arms, meanwhile, would swing on a more upright plane as the body turned. John and I enjoyed many an evening when the discussions would be on most any subject, and guaranteed to be lively and with humor. On one of those occasions, I asked him about Ben Hogan's swing. His response was short but very accurate: *"He swung everything on one plane."* That remark made in 1977 was the genesis of a very long search, which ultimately resulted in this book.

I grew up with complete admiration for both Ben Hogan and Sam Snead, especially Hogan. I was very grateful for what John had taught me. But I knew that those two heroes of my youth, plus others I had observed while playing the Tour, notably George Knudsen, did not swing in two planes. They swung everything on the same plane. Through John's generosity I knew pretty much everything about a two-plane swing but knew nothing about the one-plane swing. There was only one book that was the guidepost to it, Ben Hogan's *Five Lessons: The Modern Fundamentals of Golf*. However, it wasn't until many years—and an incredible number of failures—later that I came to understand that there were flaws in the book. There were some very major flaws, and my challenge was to sort them out.

Along the way, while searching for the perfect swings, I came to realize that all golf swings techniques, no matter how varied, fell into one of two categories. You either swing your arms in somewhat the same plane as you turn your body, or you don't. It became that simple. If your arms swing up from address to around your body on about the same plane as your shoulders turn, I call that the one-plane technique. If your arms tend to swing up more vertically, not in the same plane as your shoulders turn, but on a steeper plane, I call that the two-plane technique. It's that simple.

Another remarkable thing I discovered over the years was that what you were doing in one type of swing, you were doing nearly the opposite of in the other. The notion that there was only one set of universal fundamentals that applied to all golf swings was suddenly thrown out the window. The goal of this book is to set all of that straight.

There are two distinctly different sets of fundamentals that govern the two different types of swings. Furthermore, if you are using one type of swing and suddenly introduce an element from the other type, a breakdown occurs. The swing that used to work for you (at least most of the time) now does not work.

As a group, golfers aren't improving, even with computers, video, and a lot of very smart and dedicated teachers. I think that more people are now being hurt by information than ever before. A lot of it is because of the speed at which we can be exposed to great amounts of information. The Golf Channel, golf telecasts, lessons, the print media—all of it can deliver information at dizzying speeds. Some of it is wrong, and most of it is, at the very least, contradictory. Listen closely and you will understand just how contradictory the information is. The problem is that no one has ever before introduced the notion that there are *two* sets of fundamentals in golf, not one. Most all of the apparent contradictions are explainable if separated into the two sets of fundamentals.

I have a number of goals for this book, but none of them is more important than that of ending a great deal of the confusion about the golf swing. I want golfers to use this book so they will have a clear understanding of exactly how they can improve. Towards that end, there are several important things I hope that you will learn from reading this book. I want you to understand that many of the things that you have heard and even, perhaps, hold as universal fundamentals, are erroneous. They are not just wrong in the one-plane swing but in the two-plane swing as well. I will show you how they are completely against the very nature of what you are trying to do in the golf swing and how destructive they are. What information is left over, regardless of how seemingly contradictory, will apply to one of the two sets of fundamentals. Let me explain.

Once you determine which swing type you use, or want to use, then you will discover the fundamentals that pertain to your swing method. When you learn to discard those elements that do not fit your style and adopt those that do, you can begin to practice effectively. Golf is hard enough without practicing things that will do you no good or cause you harm. If you are only practicing those things that will be successful for you, then you cannot fail to improve. I personally have tried everything in this book, and I have also successfully taught everything in this book to others, both amateurs and professionals.

As I have pointed out, the central focal point of *The Plane Truth for Golfers* and my instructional theories revolve around the two distinctly different swing types that can occur in golf—the one-plane and two-plane swings—and the sets of fundamentals that govern each. I will thoroughly explore both swings along with a specific set of fundamentals governing each. I'll describe each of these techniques in Chapter 1, so you can start thinking about selecting the swing most suited to you. But, after this preview, I'll go into much more detail, so by the time you finish the book you'll know for sure which technique to practice.

As you will learn in Chapter 2, each of these two swings is prompted by a particular address position. For example, the one-plane swinger must bend over more at address, while the two-plane swinger promotes the correct action by standing more erect. You'll see too, that there are further differences relative to grip, stance, ball position, and weight distribution. Chapters 3 and 4 cover the swing itself. You will learn in detail the fundamentals that govern each technique during the backswing, down through impact and on into the follow-through. You will be amazed at the opposite characteristics that the two swings exhibit. You'll see the errors you have made and learn why your earlier efforts failed. You now will be able to practice in the right way and open the door to lasting improvement.

In reading *The Plane Truth for Golfers*, first decide which swing is right for you. Next, understand the fundamentals and mechanics that apply to your address, backswing, and downswing techniques by carefully reading the instructional text and studying the accompanying photographs of me, as well as those of my star student, Peter Jacobsen, so you get a clear visual picture of each and every important movement relative to *your* swing. Peter demonstrates both the one- and two-plane swings in this book's color insert.

Finally, work on the practice drills I provide in Chapter 5 so that you groove the critical actions separately before finally blending them into a single, uninterrupted flowing one-plane or two-plane golf swing that you can confidently and consistently repeat. I strongly urge you to read and study the drills section for your swing type. I present information there that is not in any other part of the book. That information is vital to your understanding and improvement.

In your quest to learn the game from scratch or trade in your existing old swing for a new one, you'll be surprised how quickly you will get results. In fact it should be almost immediate. This is not cockiness on my part. I'm telling you this fact, based on my successful experiences teaching both amateur golfers and seasoned Tour pros who came to me confused and worried that they were going to need to spend hours and hours revamping their swing in order to retrieve their game. You will not need to practice extra hard to improve, provided you select the right swing and practice the proper actions associated with it. Make the right choice, groove the proper movements, and in a short time your swing will operate efficiently.

The flight of the ball will be your guide. If you are doing something better, the ball is doing something better. If the flight of your ball does not improve, it means you do not understand the instruction clearly, you are not doing what you are being asked to do, or what you are being asked to do is wrong. Unfortunately, this last case too often has been the problem. After reading this book you will no longer have that one to worry about. You should have a crystal-clear understanding of what you need to do to improve.

Finally, how do you know if you are doing it right? Well, as said above, the golf ball tells all. If you start hitting powerfully accurate shots, you know you are on the right track. If, on the other hand, your ball flight is weak and your shots miss the target, either reread the instructions or find a video camera and see for yourself. I'll leave you with a story that illustrates that point.

Several years ago, a good friend of mine, Sam Ainslie, was invited to play golf in Texas, tour the Ben Hogan golf equipment factory in Fort Worth, and meet and have dinner with Ben Hogan. Sam got to sit next to Ben Hogan at dinner that evening and in the course of conversation Ben Hogan asked: "Do you use video?" Sam replied that he only used it on some of his students. To which Hogan said, "No, I mean, do you use video on your own game?" Sam admitted that he did not as he was a "feel" player. Hogan simply said: "Well son, if they had had video in my day, I'd have really killed them."

Let's go to the practice tee and start today's lesson.

1

The Choice Is Yours

Why you should commit to improving your

technique and the critical factors for

determining whether you are a one-plane or

two-plane swinger

Before you undertake determining which swing type and set of fundamentals is right for you, I feel some background on many of the terms and concepts that you will be studying is in order. First, though, allow me to take you back to a beginning point. I paraphrased from John Jacobs in the introduction: "The sole purpose of the golf swing is to produce a correct, repetitive impact, and the method employed is of no significance as long as it is repetitive."

We have all hit very good golf shots. All of us have—even the highest handicapper. At some point, even if by accident, we have managed to get the club into the back of the ball and going in the right direction. Hitting a good shot is a lot of fun, but unfortunately it is not something average golfers repeat with consistency. Nearly all of those out-of-the-blue good shots are a result of somehow getting the impact right. We were so far out of position in the golf swing, but still somehow found the correct impact position.

Almost none of us, if we are far out of position, are good enough athletes to find a correct repetitive impact. The only way to accomplish this goal is to be less out of position. The less out of position, the easier it is to find impact, correctly and repetitively. What *less out of position* means in golf terms is to be *on plane*. Actually, I'm a little more forgiving than saying everyone has to be exactly on plane. If you can swing on a reasonable plane and in a reasonable direction, you can play very good golf repetitively. If you bought this book thinking that I am going to dissect and detail swing technique down to the last degree of angle and centimeter of move, then you will be disappointed. I can do that, but it is a waste of time and is not productive for playing good golf. In golf, we just have to come close enough to both the plane and the direction of the plane to be able to play wonderfully. So now let's understand what the plane is.

You may have heard of shaft planes, address position planes, and swing planes. The plane I'm referring to here is the swing plane the club generally moves through from the ball at address, to the top of the backswing, and then back down to the ball and into the follow-through. All swing planes in golf contain two ingredients that make up the plane because of where the ball is located in relation to you, the golfer. It is located in two reference points relative to you. One, the ball is on the ground, and two, it is beside you. Let's look at these issues one at a time.

We will first study the fact that the ball is beside you. All endeavors where a ball is to be hit, thrown, rolled, shot, or kicked, can be divided into two groups. One group, which is not golf, I call on-line games. This is where you and the object are both located on the target line. Throwing darts, shuffleboard, bowling, shooting pool, croquet, and shooting a basketball are all on-line games in that you are standing on the target line, and the object to be hit, thrown, kicked, shot, or rolled is also on the target line. The motion in all on-line games is pretty much straight back and straight through. It doesn't matter if the object and the motion are at head level like basketball and darts, at ground level like shuffleboard, or in between like pool, the motion is in a straight line.

The other relationship that can exist is what I call side-on, where you are to the side of the target line and the object to be hit, shot, etc., is either on the line or will be released on the line. Hockey, polo, baseball, tennis, golf, and throwing a discus are all side-on endeavors. These side-on activities all have a circular nature. We are to the side of the object. The object is over there on the target line and we are to the side of it. We must swing from us, out to object, and then back again. The swing has to go in a circle; it cannot go any other way. So one of the elements in the planes of *all* golf swings is circular. You will hear this frequently throughout this book. If anyone tells you to swing on a straight line, ignore them. Trying to swing down the line as a far as possible is dangerous to the health of your golf game. Straight lines and golf do not mix. Granted, maybe for a six-inch putt—but beyond that, no. It is against the nature of golf, a side-on game, to ever go in a straight line.

Having now covered one of the two natures of the plane, circular motion, let's look at the other plane ingredient. It pertains to the fact that the ball is on the ground. If the ball were, say, waist high, then there would be only one-plane ingredient, a somewhat level circle, and a baseball swing would be the order of the day. However, the ball isn't waist high, it's on the ground, and because our shoulders and arms are where they are we must swing the club into the air and back down to the ground to effectively hit the object with any force. So the second part of a plane involves the up-and-down element. Together, these two elements—circular and up and down—form a plane. In the backswing as you go around, you also go up to form the backswing plane. As you come down, you return around to impact for the downswing plane and then back up and around for the follow through. This blend of around and up and down is essentially the golf swing. The more you go up and down and the less you go around, the more upright your plane is said to be. Conversely, the more you go around, and the less you go up and down, the flatter the plane.

Now that you understand the plane, let's look at the direction of a plane. This part is rather simple. You want the plane pointed in such a way that at impact it is swinging towards your target. If it isn't, it's either swinging too much to the right (in-to-out) or to the left (out-to-in). You don't have to be exact. In fact, many great players do not establish a plane that swings exactly at their target. The point here is to understand that there is a plane comprised of two elements and it has a direction. Again, if you can get close enough to a good plane and swing in a reasonable direction you can play good golf.

Let's next look at the fact that there are only two ways you can swing a club on plane—which is at the heart of the book you now hold in your hands. All golf swings fall into one of two different types. To understand that, let's examine how your body works as it tries to swing on an around and up-and-down plane.

Every time you turn your shoulders around your spine they move in a plane. If you are standing erect, the plane the shoulders turn in will be parallel to the ground. The more you bend over from the hips and waist and turn your shoulders around your spine, the more vertical your shoulder plane will be. The erect posture, level turn, would look like a merry-go-round, shoulder high, while the other, if bent over at 90 degrees, would look like a Ferris wheel. Having understood that, there are only two options for your arms to swing in relation to your shoulders. The arms can either swing up and onto the same plane that the shoulders are turning on, or they will swing up and onto a different plane. That really takes care of all swings. Either the arms swing somewhat on the same plane as the shoulders are turning or they do not. I call the one in which the arms swing in the same plane as the shoulders, the *one-plane swing*, and the one in which the arms and shoulders move in different planes, the *two-plane swing*.

The one-plane swing is best envisioned as a baseball swing at the ground. The spine is bent over, the shoulders are turning on an inclined plane, and the arms are swinging across and around the chest. Ernie Els is a "pure" one planer as is the teenage phenomenon Michelle Wie. Other one-plane swingers include legends Ben Hogan and Sam Snead, Chad Campbell, and Tiger Woods—although Tiger is currently undergoing some swing changes, and which type he eventually ends up with is yet to be determined.

The two-plane swinger stands fairly erect, turns fairly level to the ground, and swings the arms in a fairly vertical manner. Golf legend Tom Watson is the most pure of all two-plane swingers. Other good pro examples include David Toms, Davis Love, Karrie Webb, Nancy Lopez, and Hale Irwin.

Photos 1.1–1.3 One-plane golfers turn their shoulders around a bent-over spine and swing their arms around their upper torso onto the same plane as the shoulder turn.

The one- and two-plane swings are very different, indeed, and in some aspects opposite. The fundamentals that govern them are very different, too. It's the reason for this book. There is not one set of fundamentals that govern all golf swings, but *two* and they are distinctly different. The elements of one swing do not work in the other swing. It's why I say with great conviction, that if you are not improving in your golf, it's probably not your fault. You have been practicing the wrong fundamentals for your swing. Eliminating those wrong fundamentals and

Photos 1.4–1.6 **Two-plane golfers swing the arms on an upright angle or plane, while the shoulders turn on a flatter angle.**

just working on the right ones is the key to immediate and lasting improvement.

In the upcoming chapters, I cover the entire swing from address through to the end of the swing for both the one-plane and the two-plane techniques. Right now, though, I want to give you some of the individual characteristics for the two swings, so you can choose the best swing technique for you.

The first of those traits is that the two-plane swing is more upright than the one-plane swing. This is very important. The fact that a two-plane swing is somewhat upright and the one-plane swing is somewhat flatter will resonate throughout the book.

To look at the characteristic differences between the upright swing type and the flatter swing type, imagine a tire on your automobile as it stands upright or vertical to the ground. The tire tread will rise up off the ground the quickest, with the least amount of tire on or near the ground in this vertical position. Next, imagine as you lean the tire over, more toward lying on its side, you can observe that the sides of the tire now come up off the ground slower and more gently. More of the tire is on the ground and a lot more is very close to the ground as it curves away.

These two extreme demonstrations illustrate one of the most important differences in the two swing characteristics. The upright tire, with
the sides coming up quickly and little of the tire in touch with the
ground, has in golf terms a very unforgiving impact area. If a club were
swung in this manner it would be going down one instant and then back
up the next instant and only along the ground for such a small moment
that it would be nearly impossible to get it into the back of the ball. That
swing in golf terms is too narrow and too steep. Conversely, the tire that
is nearly lying on its side is along the ground for such a long time that
it could be viewed in terms of too wide or too shallow.

Although the two-plane swing is certainly not as vertical as in the tire
illustration, neither is the one-plane swing as flat as the tire that is nearly
leaned over on the ground. *However, the tire visual serves the purpose
to show you how the two-plane swing, which is somewhat upright, tends
to lack width and is a little too steep and too narrow. The leaned-over
tire, conversely, shows the attributes of a one-plane swing that tends to
be too flat and too shallow.* Remember these traits because they will fig-
ure prominently in your understanding of the two sets of fundamentals!

Another characteristic of the two swing types is in how they make
the plane. The one-plane swing golfer forms his plane by bending over
and, as mentioned, playing baseball off the ground. The shoulders, arms,
and the club all turn and swing around the bent-over spine angle onto
the same plane.

When you bend over, your shoulders and hips are not in the same
plane. Your hips are on top of two vertical pegs (your legs) while your
shoulders are going to turn around in an inclined spine. When you turn
these two body parts, you are actually turning them to a degree against
each other. This windup is a source of tremendous power but does
require strength and flexibility to achieve. Furthermore, this winding
and unwinding of power in the trunk of the body requires fairly strong
legs as well to stabilize the swing. So in choosing the swing to go with,
take these facts into consideration.

The two-plane swing involves doing two things simultaneously that
produce the plane. The up and down swinging arms are on a plane to
drive a tent peg into the ground. The shoulders are on a plane to hit a
baseball chest-to-waist high. The plane is a compromise between the ver-

Photos 1.7–1.9 **Body flexibility and physical strength are required for the one-plane swinger looking to hit the ball powerfully and accurately, as this sequence of photographs shows.**

tical arm swing and the horizontal shoulder turn. If you move your arms up in front of you, at exactly the same time and rate as you turn the shoulders, you will form the perfect plane. However, to accomplish this goal, timing, tempo, and rhythm are paramount. Without them, you will either be in the wrong plane or the wrong direction. This should tell you, if you are considering this two-plane method, you must have a good sense of timing and rhythm.

Both the one and the two-plane swings are good swings, but in making your choice you must assess your hand-eye coordination, flexibility, and athletic ability. Specifically, if you are flexible, strong in the chest, abdominal, back, and shoulder muscles, and aggressive too, the one-plane swing will suit you better. On the other hand, if you lack body or arm strength, and are not flexible, coordinated, and a good dancer, the two-plane action should be your choice of swing.

Because we'll be talking about impact throughout this book, this is probably the best time to address another issue that is always in the minds of avid golfers: Distance. Well, let me tell you something that most golfers don't realize. Distance is not solely a result of generating tremendous clubhead speed. It comes from the combination of clubhead speed with a level, square hit by the center of the clubface to the back of the ball. You'll find that if you begin hitting the ball consistently solid, you will obtain an increase in distance on all your full shots. It doesn't matter if you swing your driver at 80 mph at impact, 100 mph, or 120 mph. Relative to whatever speed your body can generate, you will hit the ball much farther than you thought you could. Aside from this fact, if you learn to execute either the one- or two-plane swings effectively, you will gain some additional distance because you'll be applying your energy more efficiently. So, your raw clubhead speed will increase, too. Learn the mechanics of the right swing type for you, work on making that swing a repeating motion, and you'll hit the ball much farther as well as much straighter.

Let me make one last point on this subject. People ask me, "Which method, a one-plane or two-plane swing, will hit the ball the farthest?" That is an interesting question, but there is no set answer to it. It depends on how well any given individual can implement the chosen swing mechanics.

The one-plane swing, which employs the winding of the upper body against the hips, is very powerful because the upper body recoils explo-

Photos 1.10–1.12 **The two-plane swing must depend more on timing, particularly in swinging the club from the top (left), down toward the ball (center), and through the impact zone (right).**

sively from the tensed condition of the lower spine at the top of the backswing. This explosiveness is why so many golf fans marveled at how far Ben Hogan could hit the ball. Hogan was a fairly small man and, later in his career, his swing action looked very tight and controlled. Yet the ball came off the clubface like a rifle shot. Hogan used one-plane mechanics to virtual perfection and was rewarded with great distance along with uncanny control. Still, I must warn you that the one-plane swing will not work best (or give the greatest distance) for everyone. The one-plane backswing and position at the top, in particular, require a fairly high degree of elasticity, especially in the midsection. If you are not in good condition or are elderly, the chances are that you will get more power, as well as overall effectiveness, from the two-plane action.

The two-plane swing also produces great distance in that the karate chopping motion of the arms is a very powerful lever and can generate tremendous clubhead speed. This speed and the resulting distance are by no means less than the power generated by the one-plane swing. It is, however, in my opinion, harder to hit both long and straight with the two-plane swing due to timing factors that must be considered, particularly when swinging full out. Coordinating the vertical arm swing with the horizontal shoulder turn to form a plane gets increasingly difficult as your swing spread increases. Having said that, if you devote time to learning and grooving this motion, namely through diligent practice of the drills recommended in Chapter 5, you may surprise yourself.

In the end, it does not matter to me whether you choose to become a one-plane swinger or a two-plane swinger. What does matter is this: You work only on the personal fundamentals geared to your type technique. Furthermore, right from the time you decide to embark on a swing improvement plan, you start building a solid foundation by learning how to set up according to the following specific instructions relative to either the one- or two-plane swing.

After that, it's just a matter of going with the swing that you're comfortable with and yields the best ball-flight results.

2

Getting Set

The fundamentals that govern golf's starting

position for your specific type of swing

Many golfers underestimate the importance of the address, or starting position, in golf, believing that it's okay to be idiosyncratic when it comes to such elements as grip, stance, posture, and weight distribution. However, this is simply not the case. In golf, the address is truly the engine room of the swing, because it has such a tremendous effect on the type of swing you will employ. More importantly, because the mechanics of the one-plane and two-plane swings vary, it is not only essential that you stick to the address fundamentals, but it is also critical that you focus on the ones that apply to your specific type of technique. Mixing one- and two-plane fundamentals is like mixing oil and water. Therefore you need to wipe from the chalkboard of your mind those truisms previously listed as evergreen basics—neutral grip, square stance, and balanced weight distribution. It is possible that one or two of the so-called classic fundamentals will apply to your personalized swing. If that's the case, you are ahead of the game. However, what is more important is that you become a purist and adopt *all* the fundamentals for the one-plane swing or two-plane swing that I will now map out, starting with the proper way to grip the club when addressing the ball.

Address Elements for the One-Plane Swing

Grip

Before describing the positioning of the hands on the club, let's first make sure you understand the two types of grip that I consider acceptable. The overlap grip, popularized by Harry Vardon, features a connection of the hands by the overlapping of the little finger of the right hand between the forefinger and middle finger of the left hand. The overlap is the most traditional of grip styles and is still used by the majority of better golfers. A very viable alternative is the interlock-grip style. The only difference between these two options is that in the interlock grip, instead of the little finger of the right hand overlapping the left, that finger is interlocked between the left forefinger and middle finger. Some golfers who have shorter fingers feel that this grip unifies or knits the hands a bit more securely. As long as your hands remain unified, either style could work for you.

Of greater importance than whether you overlap or interlock the fingers is the positioning of the hands in relationship to the club's handle. For the player intent on developing a one-plane swing, I advocate a grip that places the hands in a neutral-to-strong position. This means that, while the palms of the hands are facing each other, they are both turned slightly to the right, so that the back of your left hand is facing just slightly upward, as opposed to pointing directly at the target. To put it another way, the hands are considered to be in a *neutral* position if, when you look down at address, you can see two knuckles of your left hand. If you turn both hands slightly more to the right so that you can see three knuckles of your left hand, then your hands are in a *strong* position. In analyzing your grip, make sure you look straight down from the address position in order to assess your grip position correctly. So, when I say the one-plane player should have a neutral-to-strong grip, I mean

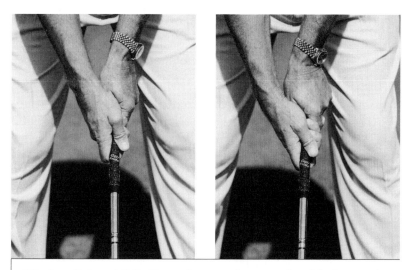

Photos 2.1 and 2.2 **One-plane swingers should choose to play with either a neutral grip (left) or a strong grip (right).**

that your hands should be positioned so that when you look down at address, you see at least two knuckles on your left hand, but never more than three knuckles.

You probably want to know why the one-plane swinger should employ a neutral-to-strong grip position. You'll understand this instructional element more fully when we discuss the action of the swing itself. However, for now, all you need to understand is that a neutral-to-strong grip, with the hands turned slightly more to the right on the handle, encourages the clubface to be more closed in relation to the path of the swing and through impact than a weaker grip would. A clubface that's slightly closed is preferable with the wider and shallower swing arc that the one-plane swing tends to produce.

Stance

For all normal full shots, from the driver through the full pitching wedge, the one-plane swinger should adopt a stance in which the feet are square to the target line or, if anything, slightly *closed* (right or rear foot is drawn back an inch or two from a line that runs parallel to your target line.) Your hips should be *square* (parallel) or slightly open to your target line. Your shoulders, meanwhile, should be square to the target

Photo 2.3 **The one-plane swinger should take a fairly wide stance, like the one shown here.**

line or, if anything, just a shade *open* (pointing slightly left of target) for those who have adopted slightly open hips.

Your stance should also be neutral to moderately wide. This means that for a full driver, the distance between your heels should be at least as wide as the shirt seams at the points of your shoulders. The stance will gradually become narrower as you work your way down through the shorter irons, until the feet are approximately 12 inches apart for a full wedge. Keep in mind, of course, that the distance between the feet will always be somewhat wider for the tall player than for the golfer of shorter stature.

I advocate a slightly wider stance for the one-plane swinger because it provides a more stable basis for the wider, flatter swing that results from the arms and shoulders turning on the same plane during the swing. The wider stance allows you to move the entire trunk or midsection as aggressively as you can, which is something you'll want to do as a one-plane swinger.

An often-overlooked issue with regards to stance is the positioning of the feet. For the one-plane swing, I recommend you point your left foot outward, toward the target, at an angle of 30 to 45 degrees. Meanwhile, your right or rear foot should be square to the target line. Positioning your feet this way is consistent with the mechanics of the one-plane swing, which we'll discuss in detail later. For now, suffice it to say that in the one-plane swing you want to build tension between the turning of your shoulders and your hips during the backswing. Keeping your left foot turned out while the right foot is set square prevents your hips from turning too far back. In addition, this stance increases the tension between your upper and lower body on the backswing, which is a desirable power-building element in the one-plane swing.

Ball Position

Most instruction regarding ball position tends to focus on the position of the ball between the feet, which we will discuss shortly. What teachers and students often overlook is the distance that the ball should be away from your feet. This is an important element of your address position, which dictates the plane of your golf swing. Basically, the closer you stand to the ball, the more upright your plane will be. The farther you stand from the ball, the flatter your swing plane. In general, the one-plane swinger should stand farther from the ball than the two-plane swinger. You'll understand why shortly when we discuss your posture. There is no one, precise or universal distance that the ball should be from your toes. It depends upon both your height and the club you're hitting. The taller you are and the longer the club, the farther you should stand from the ball to swing comfortably and ultimately hit the ball solidly. Taking these things into consideration, the one-plane swinger should stand farther from the ball than the two-plane swinger.

Unlike the issue of distance, the ball's position in terms of center alignment in relation to the feet does not differ for one-plane and two-plane swingers. This does not mean that the ball position is the same for all shots, however. For a teed-up driver, the ball should be positioned opposite a line drawn to your left heel or just slightly ahead of it, opposite your left instep. This ball position allows you to sweep the club through impact, making contact while the clubhead is just beyond its lowest point and is beginning to ascend. As the clubs get shorter and you want to strike the ball with a more descending blow, move the ball back in your stance, until it is just about in the middle or slightly back-of-middle of the narrowed stance for a full pitching wedge. Keep in mind that the ball position may also vary depending on whether course conditions call for you to hit a lower or higher shot than normal or to draw or fade the shot. To hit a low shot or a right-to-left draw, position the ball a little back from where you ordinarily would. To hit a high shot or a fade, you should position the ball a little more forward in the stance than normal.

Photo 2.4 The one-plane swinger should bend over more at address with the hands directly below the chin.

Posture

In the one-plane swing, the shoulders will turn on a more upright plane than in the two-plane swing, in which the shoulders turn more horizontally while the arm swing is more upright. This is because the shoulders turn at a 90-degree angle to the spine, and the spine is much more bent over in the one-plane swing (creating a steeper turn) than in the two-plane swing.

If you want to develop a one-plane swing, then at address you should bend over noticeably toward the ball. The taller you are, the more you should bend from the hips. Peter Jacobsen, who is 6'3" tall and who has beautifully adapted the one-plane setup and swing, uses a vivid mental image to remind himself to bend over at address. He says that once he gets his feet into position, he thinks about putting his nose on a table that's directly in front of him. You don't actually have to bend that much, but remember to bend enough so that your spine is well tilted, at least 35 to 45 degrees below vertical. Also make sure that you are slightly bent out. The more you bend out, even slightly toward the balls of your feet, the easier it will be to bring your arms in close to your body and then around your chest. Make sure that your hands are directly under your chin. Once you are in this position, you should be able to decide how far to stand from the ball.

To determine correct balance: Take your address position, then have a friend stand behind you along your target line with a yardstick in hand. He or she should then line up the top of the yardstick with the front of your shoulders and leave the bottom of the yardstick dangling. If you have bent your spine over and out enough at address, the yardstick should dangle slightly outside the toes of your shoes.

Finally, how do you know if you are bent over enough? Start by addressing the ball, bent over with your hands under your chin. Next, hold the yardstick across one shoulder so it is pointing out toward the ball. Position the yardstick so that it is at a 90-degree angle to your spine. Have your friend tell you if the yardstick is pointing into a zone that is from the ball to within four feet outside the ball (or approximately 48 inches). If the yardstick is pointing to the middle of that zone, then you are bending over the correct amount. If it is pointing to the top of the zone or outside of the zone, then you are not bending over enough. Conversely, if the yardstick is pointing at the ball or out of the zone—to the inside—you are bent over too far.

As a one-plane swinger, you should also center your weight directly over the hips, with your spine perfectly centered. You want to keep the spine centered at address because the tendency of the player who turns the arms and shoulders on a single plane is to employ a swing that is somewhat too wide and too flat. If your spine tilts to the right, you're going to have too much width in your swing.

Finally, the one-plane swinger's hands should be centered or just an inch or two ahead of the center of the body. Depending on the club being used, at address the hands will be very close to even with the club-head, neither ahead nor behind the clubhead. The one-plane swinger should never have his or her hands positioned very far in front of the clubhead for any normal full shot. You can check this by imagining a line extending out of the shaft and grip toward your torso. That line should always point somewhere between the left side of the fly of your pants and the pleat on your left pant leg. In doing this on drives with the ball played forward in the stance, your hands will be just behind the clubhead. Conversely, when hitting a wedge or short iron with the ball played back in the stance, your hands will be ahead of the clubhead.

You may recall, incidentally, that when we discussed the stance, I mentioned that the shoulders should be square to slightly open, as opposed to the feet that should be square or slightly closed to the target line. You may have wondered why this would be the case. Well, the alignment of the shoulders is related to the positioning of your hands and arms at address. With your hands nearly centered in relation to your body and your right hand below your left on the grip, it stands to reason that your right shoulder might be pulled outward just slightly, toward the ball. This means that a line drawn across your shoulders will tend to be slightly open in relation to your target line, even though your feet should be aligned square to slightly closed. To put it another way, in order to have your shoulders aligned square to the target, you will have to slightly soften or bend your right arm so that the arms are not equally straight.

Weight Distribution

At address for all normal full shots, the one-plane player should distribute his or her weight evenly, with 50 percent on each foot. Shifting your weight slightly to the balls of your feet will help make it easier to achieve the

Photo 2.5 The one-plane swinger should distribute his or her weight toward the balls of the feet to promote a comfortable outward lean.

correct amount of outward lean. This is the best way to stay in balance throughout the swinging motion.

"I feel so bent over at address that it seems that my shoulders are out in front of my feet," says PGA Tour player Paul Azinger. "I visualize myself standing on top of a 50-story building and bending out over the edge as far as I can without losing my balance."

Address Elements for the Two-Plane Swing

Grip

While I suggest a neutral-to-strong grip for the one planer, I believe that a neutral-to-weak grip is the preferred hand position for the two-plane swinger. (Whether your grip is neutral or slightly weak depends on how you naturally tend to deliver the clubface to the ball.) By neutral grip here I mean the same positioning as described for the one-plane address. You should be able to see at most two knuckles. Alternatively, if you place your hands in a fairly weak position, your hands will be shaded slightly more to the left on the club's handle so that when you look down you will see at least all the first knuckle on your left hand.

This slight difference in your hold on the club is needed because the neutral-to-weak grip encourages a clubface that's positioned square to slightly open in relation to the path of the swing. The two-plane swinger will benefit from a clubface that is slightly open. Why? Two-plane swingers tend to move the club along an arc that is more upright and steep, or less horizontal and around, than the one-plane swinger's arc. Without getting too technical, a clubface that is closed tends to steepen the angles in the golf swing. Therefore, a two-plane swing that is already somewhat too steep does not need an additional steep angle. A clubface that's moving into the ball from a more open position is easier to play with than a clubface that's more closed. So, the more open clubface that the slightly weaker grip encourages is preferable for the two-plane swinger. Therefore, make sure that, whether you overlap or interlock, you see no more than two knuckles on your left hand.

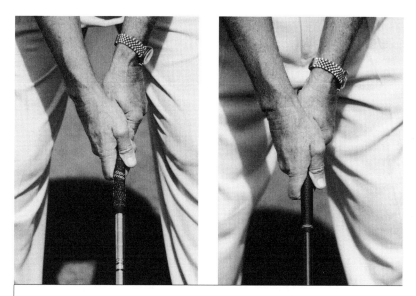

Photos 2.6 and 2.7 A neutral grip (left) or a weak grip (right) is recommended for the two-plane swinger.

Stance

A line across your toes should lie parallel to your target line or slightly right of target for all full normal shots.

The two-plane swinger should also assume a stance that, relative to the length of the club, will be of medium-to-slightly-narrow width. This means that for a driver, the distance between the feet should be narrower than the outside width of the shoulders; and for a full pitching wedge, the heels should be no more than 10 inches apart. Why, you may wonder, should the stance be a bit narrower for the two-plane player than for the one-plane player? The two-plane swing minimizes the body as a source of power and maximizes the arm swing. Standing with the feet closer together places the body in a slightly weaker, less-dominant setup. The body's primary function is to turn in response to the swing of the arms rather than to be a source of power. By keeping your stance somewhat narrow and staying on balance, your body complements the arm swing. If you have a narrow stance and your body starts to move too powerfully for the arm swing, you will quickly feel a loss of balance.

***Photo 2.8* Two-plane golfers encourage the proper swing by standing with their feet positioned relatively narrowly.**

As to the positioning of the feet, unlike with the one-plane player, I prefer to see a two-plane player point his or her left foot square to the target line. By keeping the left foot square, you'll be freer to turn your hips farther around on the backswing. This is desirable in the two-plane swing because you are trying to develop a full body turn, as opposed to developing tension between the upper and lower body. Your right foot, incidentally, should also point square to the target line.

Ball Position

First let's talk about the distance from the ball to your feet. This distance varies depending on the length of the club you're using: The basic rule of thumb here is the longer the club, the farther away you should stand from the ball. Nevertheless, two-plane swingers should stand closer to the ball for all regular shots. You'll need to stand closer, because your arm swing will be more upright than that of the one-plane player. Therefore, as you swing through the hitting area, the clubhead will not be extended out as far away from you. Naturally, you want the ball to be just far enough away from you so that the middle of your clubface meets it squarely as you swing. The checkpoint for the correct distance is the same for the two-plane swing as for the one-plane swing: Your hands should be directly under your chin with your posture fairly erect.

As to the position of the ball in the stance relative to the feet, there is no difference between the two-plane and one-plane swinger per se. The ball positions will be the same as those described above for the one-plane player. Whether you are a one-plane or two-plane hitter, those times when you position your ball differently will have to do with a special type of shot you're trying to hit or a change in club.

Posture

This is one area of the address in which the differences between the one- and two-plane players are most obvious.

When viewed from down target, the two-plane player's spine is more straight or erect than the one-plane swinger's. You should bend from the waist slightly, perhaps 10 to 20 degrees from vertical. The more erect posture pre-positions your shoulders to turn on a more horizontal plane, while the arms swing on a steeper, more tilted plane. Therefore, check your position regularly by having a friend stand behind you, on your target line, dangling a yardstick so that the top of the yardstick lines up with the front of your shoulders. Your spine angle is correct for the two-plane swing if the bottom of the yardstick dangles over your toes, rather than slightly outside your toes as for the one-plane player.

Photo 2.9 The two-plane swinger should stand fairly erect at address, with the ball positioned closer to the body.

Whereas the one-plane golfer's shoulders are directly over his or her hips and the spine is perfectly centered, the two-plane swinger's spine should be tilted about 10 degrees to the right. The right shoulder should also be quite a bit lower than the left shoulder, as opposed to their being nearly level for the one-plane player. Furthermore, the shoulders should be somewhat over the right of center of the hips, as opposed to directly over them, which is the case when the one-plane swinger sets up.

In summary, the body's posture for the two-plane swinger is not nearly as symmetrical as that of the one-plane golfer. In fact, this type of address is often referred to as the *inverted K* position. There is a nearly straight line going from the point of the player's left shoulder down through his or her left hip and left leg. This makes up the trunk or the tall line of the inverted K. Meanwhile, the right arm is angled more forward so that the right hand can meet the left hand on the club's grip. The right arm forms the angled top line of the inverted K. The right leg is more angled inward from foot to hip than it is in the one-plane address. This right-leg position forms the angled bottom line of the inverted K.

By now, I would not be at all surprised if you are wondering how an address posture that is so different, asymmetrical, and unnatural looking when compared to the posture for the one-plane swing, could possibly be correct. Well, that's an understandable question. Answering it will also bring to light more of the differences between the one-plane and two-plane swings and also explain that while I believe both techniques can be very effective, I favor the one-plane golf swing.

As I pointed out earlier, the golfer employing the two-plane swing will always tend to swing the club on a more upright and narrower arc than the one-plane swinger. The advantage of this is that the club travels on an arc that stays closer to the target line. However, because the arc is steeper, it also means that the club is moving more downward and then abruptly upwards, with less width at the bottom during impact. As a result, it is difficult to get the clubface level on impact with the back of the ball unless a widening element in the swing can be found. So two-plane players need to put themselves in positions that tend to add width to their swings. The inverted K posture, in which the right shoulder is lowered and more of the body weight is set behind the ball, helps to add the needed width.

Photo 2.10 At address, the two-plane swinger's arms should hang comfortably with the hands positioned directly under the chin.

Weight Distribution

Your weight distribution for all regular full shots should slightly favor your right or rear foot—60 percent on your right or rear leg, 40 percent on your forward leg. This weight distribution is in keeping with your setup, in which your upper body is canted to the right. This weight distribution as well as posture, in effect, predisposes you to tilt more to the right, more behind the ball during the swing, adding more width to your golf swing.

Review: One-Plane Versus Two-Plane Address

I've given you a great deal of information to digest about how the address positions differ between the one- and two-plane swings. To help avoid any confusion, I will now summarize the critical technical elements of the vital starting position (setup). These summaries include warnings that will help you avoid making the most common errors golfers commit when formulating their address.

One-Plane Address

Grip: Neutral-to-strong position, with palms facing and in a position in which you can see at least two but no more than three knuckles on the left hand.

WARNING
Do not attempt to develop a one-plane swing action while using a weak grip. A weak grip is one in which the back of the left hand directly faces the target.

Stance: Moderate-to-wide stance, with the distance between your heels at least as great as the width of your shoulders when using the driver. Feet should be aligned and parallel to the target line, or slightly closed. The left foot should be angled out 30 to 45 degrees toward the target with the right foot set square to the target line. Hips and shoulders are square to slightly open.

WARNING
Do not attempt to develop a one-plane swing action while playing from an open stance on full shots. This will force you to move the right hip in an incorrect pushing manner during the downswing as a means of starting the ball on-target. This hip movement at the expense of a free shoulder turn can quickly lead to back problems.

Ball Position: The ball should be farther from the feet for the one-plane player. Ball position in relation to the feet should be opposite the left heel or instep for a driver, dead center or slightly ahead of center for mid irons, and middle or slightly right of center for short irons and wedges.

WARNING
Do not position the ball too close to your feet. This will force you to swing your arms on an exaggeratedly steep plane, one that your shoulder turn could only match by tilting rather than turning.

Posture: Bend over more from the spine, at least 35 to 45 degrees forward from vertical and somewhat out toward the ball. Taller golfers will bend more than shorter players. A line drawn down from the shoulders should point just outside of or beyond the toes. When viewed from the front, the shoulders should be directly over the hips, and the spine should appear perfectly straight.

WARNING

Do not tilt your spine to the right at address. Doing so will unnecessarily create more width on the backswing.

Weight Distribution: On full shots, keep your weight evenly balanced, 50 percent on each foot with the weight toward the balls of your feet.

WARNING

Do not put more than 50 percent of your weight on your left foot, particularly when playing the driver and fairway woods. Doing so will result in a steeper hit and cause power to be drained from your swing.

Two-Plane Address

Grip: A neutral-to-weak position, with palms matching and in a position in which you can see at least one knuckle (but no more than two) on the left hand.

WARNING

Do not try to develop a two-plane swing while using a strong grip—i.e., a grip in which the back of the left hand points somewhat upward and one in which you can see three knuckles on that hand.

Stance: Moderate to narrow stance width. Distance between heels is slightly narrower than outside width of the shoulders when hitting a driver. Feet aligned parallel to the target line or slightly closed. Left foot set square to the target line, with right foot square to that line. Hips and shoulders are square or slightly open to the target line.

WARNING
Do not set up with a wide stance. This promotes stronger use of the body than is desired in the two-plane swing.

Ball Position: The ball should be slightly closer to the feet for the two-plane player. As with the one-plane swing, ball position in relation to the feet should be opposite left heel to instep for a driver, dead center for mid irons, and slightly right of center for short irons and wedges.

WARNING
Do not position the ball too far away from your feet. When the ball is too far away, your arms will swing on too flat a plane than needed for the two-plane swing.

Posture: Spine is more erect, bent toward the ball by no more than 20 degrees from vertical. Shorter players will be slightly more erect than taller players. A line drawn straight down from the shoulders should point to the toes. When viewed from the front, the shoulders are positioned slightly to the right of center of the hips, the right shoulder is lower than the left shoulder, and the spine is tilted slightly to the player's right.

WARNING
Do not bend over too much. Bending over too far forces you to turn your shoulders in too upright a manner for an effective two-plane swing.

Weight Distribution: Place about 60 percent of your weight on your right foot and 40 percent on your left for normal full shots.

WARNING

Do not put more than 60 percent of your weight on your rear foot, particularly on short iron shots, as it will increase the likelihood that you will hit fat and thin.

I hope that you now have a clear understanding of the differences at address for the one-plane and two-plane swings. Now we can proceed to discuss the actual motion of these two different techniques.

EQUIPMENT ADVICE

Before discussing the swing, a word about your equipment is in order. Because of the differences in posture between one- and two-plane players, the lie of your clubs is a factor you need to be aware of. (For the uninitiated, the lie of the club refers to the angle at which the club shaft is set into the hosel of the clubhead.)

The lie angle is a significant element of club fitting that most golfers overlook. If the lie is too upright for you, the club will rest on its heel, with the toe off the ground. At impact, the heel will tend to catch in the turf and close the face somewhat, sending the ball left. If the lie is too flat, the heel will be up and the opposite will tend to happen: The toe of the club may catch, which tends to open the clubface and send the ball to the right.

There is another problem that can occur when your lies are off that few are aware of. Without getting too technical, when the lie is too upright for your posture, the loft on the clubface gets turned a bit, so that it will send the ball to the left of where you believe you are aiming. Conversely, if the lie is too flat,

the loft of the club's face is turned to the right of where you're aiming, so you hit the ball right. So obviously it is important that the lie of your clubs fits your address position. The one-plane player, who will be bent over and standing a little farther from the ball on average, will need a lie that is slightly flatter than average. How much flatter will also depend on your height: If you're tall, you might need only a small adjustment from standard. If you are a short one-plane player, however, you might need to flatten your lie angle two or more degrees. (For example Ben Hogan, who stood 5'8" and was a model one-plane swinger, had lies that were significantly flatter than average.)

Conversely, the two-plane player, particularly the taller player, is likely to need a lie that is a bit more upright than standard. So if you adjust your set-up posture after reading this book, be aware that you may need to adjust the lie of your clubs as well. Ask a golf professional to look at your clubs and check the lie angles. Unless a radical change in angle is required, they can be usually be adjusted (bent) to fit your setup.

3

Get Going

The proven backswing fundamentals for the one-plane swing are much different than those for the two-plane swing

If you regularly read golf magazines, take lessons, or watch The Golf Channel, you probably believe that the following are the most important basics or fundamentals concerning one's ability to employ the perfect backswing action:

1. Make a sweeping, one-piece take-away, controlled by the arms and shoulders, keeping the wrists quiet.
2. Turn your shoulders at a 90-degree angle to your spine, making sure to rotate your left shoulder under your chin.
3. Shift 60 percent of your body weight onto your right foot and leg.
4. Keep your arms in front of you.

5. Turn your hips 45 degrees.
6. Maintain your spine angle.
7. Keep your head steady.

I admit that at one time I believed these and other "tried-and-true" basics that were supposedly followed by all great players. Frankly, though, trusting in these supposed fundamentals was the chief reason I never reached my full potential as a player. I only discovered the false-hoods after tireless research and have since concluded that there is not, in fact, *one* set of fundamentals. But rather, there are *two*—those relating to the one- and two-plane swings.

By the time I woke up to reality, it was too late for me to use what I had learned to become a successful tour player. Time had certainly passed me by, and, besides that, I had already switched professions and had become a teacher and golf course designer. That's the bad news. The good news is that it's not too late for you to learn from the following clear-cut, proven fundamentals that will help you become either a one- or two-plane pure swinger.

Executing the One-Plane Backswing

Before we begin exploring the swing in detail, let me reiterate that it is not my intention to define the absolutely perfect golf swing. Nor do I believe that you, or any golfer for that matter, should expect to make an absolutely perfect golf swing every time. That applies to Tiger Woods as much as it applies to you. In golf, as in any sport, there is no such thing as perfection of execution. Take such basketball greats as Magic Johnson, Larry Bird, Kareem Abdul-Jabbar, and Michael Jordan. I can assure you that each of these players missed thousands of shots, even uncontested ones. In golf, perfection would mean a player would shoot an 18-hole score of 32 on a regulation par-72 course. That would require the player to hit every shot in the hole whenever the hole is in reach (i.e., a hole-in-one on each par-three hole, and holing out in two shots on every par-four and par-five hole).

Now, with the tremendous advances in talent, equipment, coaching, and physical training that are taking place not only on the PGA Tour but worldwide, I believe that, 20 or even 10 years from now, there might be scoring that we can't conceive of today. But no one will ever shoot a 32 on a par-72 course, because there never will be such a thing as perfection in any athletic endeavor.

Of course, every golfer should strive to improve every time he or she tees up, whether for a round or a practice session. But to get back to my purpose here, I want to explain the two distinct methods of building a functional golf swing. I will start by defining what a functional swing is. By functional swing I mean a swing that allows you to hit the ball with accuracy and for good distance so that you can reliably hit a high percentage of fairways from the tee and greens in regulation. This requires that you, first, swing the club on a reasonably good, consistent plane around you, and second, swing the clubhead so that it is moving in an accurate direction (i.e. toward the intended target) at the instant when it meets the ball. As with the elements of the address, let's take a careful look at how to build a sound backswing using the one-plane swing method.

Shoulders

The plane of the swing is an imaginary line or panel, if you will, that runs upward on an angle from the golf ball to your shoulders at address, and then continues up behind you. As mentioned earlier, it contains two directional elements—around and up/down. In order to swing successfully using a one-plane swing, you must learn to turn both your shoulders and your torso, as well as swing your arms and the golf club around, as closely as possible to this ideal plane. Now, as I stated earlier, there is no such thing as perfection in the golf swing. I have found that you can hit excellent shots as long as you keep the turn of your shoulders and torso close to the plane I've described. If anything, I would like to see your shoulders turn on a plane that is a little flatter at address than the plane from your shoulders to the ball. This would mean that when your shoulders reached the top of the backswing, they would point somewhere within a zone extending from the ball to slightly beyond it. I first mentioned this zone in the last chapter when discussing posture in the one-plane swing.

One reason I am an advocate of the one-plane golf swing is that it has fewer moving parts. *One plane* means that the shoulders, the arms, and the club shaft are all swung up and onto the single plane line as I've

INCH-BY-INCH DRILL

This drill will help you get the feel of the type of shoulder turn I'm advocating.

Take your normal address position with, say, a five-iron or fairway-metal club. While staying in the address position, pick up the club and hold it horizontally along the front of your shoulders. Next, turn your shoulders 90 degrees as you would to make a complete backswing. Have a friend stand behind you, along the target line, so he or she can tell you where the butt of the club is pointing. If it is pointing close to the middle of a zone anywhere from the ball to within 48 inches beyond it, you are turning your shoulders on a very acceptable plane for the one-plane golf swing.

Practice this drill indoors or out whenever you get the chance, particularly if at first your shoulder turn is outside or toward the outside of the limits. Any change in the angle of the shoulder turn will feel uncomfortable if you have been turning your shoulders at a different angle for a long time. Stick with it! If I had to choose one thing I would like to see any one-plane golfer, amateur or professional, do correctly it would be to turn the shoulders on a good, consistent plane every time.

described. However, now might be a good time to mention that the one-plane swing requires somewhat more athleticism of the golfer than does the two-plane swing. More athleticism is required because, when you bend from the hips at address, it means that your shoulders (as well as your arms and the club) will be turning on a different axis from that of your hips. That is, your shoulders will be turning more vertically than your hips. This creates tension in the muscles in your torso that only increases as you turn back to the top of the swing. To execute the one-plane golf swing, you have to be supple enough so that you can stretch or coil the shoulders and torso, which are tilted forward, against the lower torso and the hips, which are more upright. Ideally, you should turn your shoulders 90 degrees or more from where they were in the address position.

To get the feeling of turning your upper torso only, stand upright, with the front of your thighs against the edge of a table or desk. While keeping your legs in contact with the desk, simulate a backswing by turning your shoulders as far to the right as you can. If you can turn your shoulders 60 to 70 degrees while keeping the front of your legs against

Photo 3.1 **This Inch-by-Inch Drill is ideal for getting a feel for the shoulder-turn plane I'm advocating.**

the table, you possess the needed suppleness to make the one-plane swing work for you.

Next, stand upright with no "props," again simulating a backswing by turning your shoulders to the right as far as you can while keeping your hips in place. Can you feel a stretching of the muscles along the base of your spine? If so, that's good. Now turn your shoulders as fully as you can back to the left, as in your follow-through. You should feel that same tension. Now repeat the drill, only this time bend from the waist as you would at address before making your turn in both directions. You are gradually learning how to turn your upper body independently of your lower body, as you must to become a one-plane player.

Sometimes visualizing the plane can help you learn the movement of your shoulders along this plane. So heed these instructions. As you stand at address, you are bent over 35 to 45 degrees. As you turn on the backswing, visualize the right shoulder going up and behind you while the left shoulder moves down and in front of you. Similarly, when you turn in the downswing, let the right shoulder go down and out toward the ball and the left shoulder move up and away from the target line. Finally, in the follow-through, the right shoulder should continue to move down and in front of you while the left shoulder moves up and behind you on your left side.

Visualizing the plane positions and practicing them along with the earlier Inch-by-Inch Drill or with the On-Plane Shoulder Turn Drill in Chapter 5, will be very beneficial for feeling the plane.

Arms

As I mentioned in Chapter 1, the one-plane golf swing is something like hitting a baseball. Now, let me go into more detail. The main difference is that in baseball, you're swinging a bat at a pitch that's between knee and chest high. In golf, your swing must deliver the club to the back of a ball resting on the ground (or just off the ground, on a tee). In the baseball swing and the one-plane golf swing, the arms move very similarly; they move around your chest. In a one-plane backswing, the arms move slightly up from address and as far across and around your chest as possible; and on the through-swing they again move as far across and around your chest as possible. Now, I realize that this arm movement is inconsistent with recent thought that you should always keep your arms in front of you. That is very good advice for a two-plane swing, but it is disastrous for the one-plane golfer. On the backswing, the left arm should swing inward and directly across the chest as it does when the baseball player cocks the bat prior to stepping into the pitch. Your left arm should swing in and back onto the same plane as your shoulders are turning and should stay in contact with the chest not only on the backswing but throughout the downswing until just before impact when the arms start to swing back across the chest. The left arm will also remain straight, although not rigid, throughout the backswing.

Here's another teaching tip for you to try, which I gave to Peter Jacobsen when we first started working together. It's also one you might see Scott McCarron use on the practice range or even between shots during a tournament. Take a small towel or a head-cover. Insert it under your left upper arm and try to hold it in place as you make short back- and through-swings. As you get used to holding the object in place under your arm, gradually extend the length of your swings in each direction. If your left arm acts like that of most golfers, you'll probably find it difficult to hold the item in place. Keep working at it, though, and you'll get the feeling of your upper left arm being pinned across your chest throughout the backswing and into the follow-through. This practice exercise teaches you to keep your body in control of your swing, with your left arm simply going along with your body.

As you turn past the midway point in the backswing, your left forearm should begin to turn in a clockwise motion so that the back of the forearm faces the sky. This pronation of the forearm allows you to set the club shaft and the clubhead behind you while keeping it moving on the same plane as your arm and shoulders. Practice this pronating move in front of a mirror as you complete the final one-third of the backswing.

We've been talking only about the movement of your left arm to this point. As for your right or rear arm, it should be folding up and behind you, with the elbow moving along a plane parallel to the turn of your torso

Photo 3.2 Here we see how the left arm moves in the backswing, with its upper biceps area hugging the chest.

and your shoulders. Your right elbow, incidentally, should stay slightly away from the body until you reach the top of the backswing. At this point the pronating movement of your left arm may bring the right elbow in closer. However, you should not pin your elbow tightly against your side, as you may have read in other publications. Pinning your elbow to your side could force your left arm to swing on too flat a plane. By the same token, the right elbow should not point directly downward at the top of the backswing. Rather, it should point out and away from the body or behind you. Ideally, the right arm, from the elbow to the shoulder, should be on a line pointing behind you that mirrors the bent-over angle of the spine. In fact, if you are going to make a mistake, I'd much rather see you point the right elbow more behind the body. When the elbow points well away from you, it's referred to in teaching circles as a "flying right elbow," which most teachers will tell you is a serious flaw. It isn't a serious flaw, though, and—as noted—some pretty fair professional "hybrid" swingers exaggerate the flying right elbow position— John Daly, Fred Couples, Jack Nicklaus in his prime years, Miller

Photo 3.3 Here we see how, in the one-plane swing, the right elbow moves up and behind the body. It is permissible for the one-plane golfer to allow his or her right elbow to point farther outward, with the club arriving in a slightly laid-off position.

Barber, Gay Brewer, and even Byron Nelson. I believe it is much easier to drop the right arm slightly at the start of the downswing (as you would if the elbow flies a bit) than it is to lift it free of the body after having kept it in tightly throughout the backswing. But, again, keeping the right arm and elbow slightly free of the body and pointing behind you at least on the same line as the angle of your spine rather than straight down would be best of all.

"I feel my right elbow go immediately up and behind me, pulling my left arm into my chest," says PGA Tour player Tom Pernice, Jr. "It feels like my arms are far more inside and narrower than ever before."

One last word on the right arm: Many golfers cock the club too upright, off plane, with the right arm and hand as they pronate the left arm. Despite the efforts of the left arm to set the club on plane, the right arm and hand do not cooperate and instead lift the club's shaft above the plane and "across the line." For these golfers, I suggest they also rotate the right forearm and wrist clockwise while rotating the left forearm. The feeling will be that the back of the right hand is turning and facing directly away from the target at the top of the backswing. A note of caution: Too much rotation of either forearm can result in the opposite condition, that of a club that can be too far beneath the plane, or "laid off." However, if the club is not exactly right and on plane, then it is preferable for a one-plane swinger to have the club pointed slightly left.

"After my left arm is pinned to my chest. . . I complete my backswing by turning my right wrist and forearm clockwise to set the club on plane," says PGA Tour player Brad Faxon. "I feel very low and deep with my arms, and laid off too."

Hips

The role of the hips in the one-plane swing is very different from their role in the two-plane swing. The one-plane swing actually loads torque from a maximum shoulder turn against the lower torso and hips, which you would like to have remain as stable as possible. For an effective and powerful one-plane swing, you need to turn your shoulders at least 90 degrees, while at the same time limiting the turning of your hips to 45 degrees or less. This would give you a differential of at least 45 degrees between the amount of your shoulders' turn and that of your hips.

You are coiling your upper body against your lower body like a spring. If you do this correctly, not only will you build tremendous power, but you will also find that the downswing begins automatically with the release of this pent-up tension between your upper and lower torsos, as well as your hips. When the hips do turn, they are somewhat affected by the movement of the shoulders, even though the hips and shoulders are not on the same plane. The hips are above your legs and on a fairly level plane. The shoulders are on a much steeper plane. Furthermore, the steeper turning of the shoulders around the bent-over spine will pull the hips slightly out of a level position as they turn.

The hips end up on a tilted plane, which is about halfway between that of the shoulders and level to the ground. As the left hip turns, it goes down slightly in the backswing. This is a result of the dominating shoulder turn. Do not fight this natural tilt. Allow the hips to be influenced by the shoulders rather than actually forcing the hips into a turn. As you swing, practice keeping the hips subject to the turn of the shoulders. The more you work at it, the greater the tension you will build into your backswing turn.

A word is necessary here about the role of the right leg during the backswing. As you execute the one-plane backswing, keep your right or rear leg angled inward at least as much as it was angled in at address. You never want your right leg to sway or buckle outward as you continue to swing back. This is a very common flaw among golfers of all ability levels, but it is particularly damaging to the one-plane swinger. That's because when your right leg sways back, your lower body tends to go with it and your upper body often leans left. When this happens, you'll drastically narrow the width of the backswing. Remember, in the one-plane swing you do *not* want extra width. However, you do not want to make a move, even if it is a narrowing one that would drastically affect the swing. Sometimes when the lower body moves to the right the upper body moves to the right along with it. When that happens you get even wider and a one-plane swing that already tends to be too wide now becomes so wide and shallow that you'll be prone to hitting a weak, fat shot or a low-flying, thin shot. Sometimes too much grass will intervene between the clubhead and the ball on fairway shots, resulting in a flyer. When you hit one of these shots, you lose control of your distance. So keep your right leg angled in, which will help keep your hips centered over the ball throughout the backswing motion. If anything, I would rather see the one-plane swinger increase the amount that his or her right leg is angled in. This is unusual advice, I know, because too much of an increase in this angle can sometimes result in a reverse weight shift at the top. But I firmly believe you're better off with a tiny bit of reverse weight shift than you would be if you allowed that right leg sag outward.

Let me make one other point about the right leg. As a one-plane swinger, it's mandatory that during the backswing you maintain the same slight flex in your right knee that you started with at address. The knee can straighten up a little but never allow it to fully straighten and lock. Allowing your right knee to straighten can negatively affect your ability to turn in the downswing. It's very helpful, by the way, to have a spotter behind you, watching your right knee as you practice your backswing. If your spotter kneels behind you so his or her eyes are nearly level with your knee, then he or she will be more likely to detect it if your right knee straightens or locks. It also helps if you wear shorts during this exercise, so the viewer can get a perfectly clear view of what the knee joint is doing as you swing back.

Photo 3.4 In swinging back, the one-plane swinger should turn the shoulders fairly vigorously while limiting hip turn, promoting torque and power.

Spine

In the one-plane backswing, it is critical that your spine remains centered over the ball and does not move upward. When viewed face-on, the spine should never drift to the right as you swing back, which is a very common flaw, even among professional golfers. In fact, with this swing method I would even say that it's all right if your spine were to tilt just slightly in the opposite direction, that is, toward the target. Many teachers would argue that any tilting of the spine toward the target, no matter how small, results in a reverse weight shift, and technically they would be correct. However, I contend that a slight spine tilt to the left as you reach the top is not harmful, as again this serves to limit the width of your swing. I might add that none other than Ben Hogan, widely agreed to have the most efficient swing of his era (if not of all time), had the slightest of spine tilts toward the target at the top of his backswing. Among modern-era players, David Duval in his prime had some target-ward spine tilt at the top. So you'll be in the best shape if, during the entire backswing, you keep your spine as close to centered with no tilt right. And, incidentally, when you accomplish this, your head will remain centered above your stance, with your shoulders turning around the fixed point at the nape of your neck.

Photo 3.5 Ideally, during the backswing, the one-plane golfer's spine angle should remain constant and centered, with a limited amount of weight being transferred to the right foot and leg. In fact, even when reaching the top, weight should be balanced on both feet or favor the left foot.

What about the forward-bending angle of the spine during the backswing, as viewed from down target? You would like to keep the spine angle constant throughout the swing, of course. For one-plane players, it is a critical error to raise your head and decrease your spine angle on the backswing. If you do, it will cause your shoulder plane to become too flat or outside the shoulder plane zone. You must then lower your spine angle on the downswing precisely as much as you raised it going back.

Before moving on, let me make sure you understand where I'm going with my instructional logic. Raising the spine angle during the swing is probably the most harmful mistake the one-plane player can make, whereas lowering the spine or slightly increasing the spine angle is okay. The great Ben Hogan lowered his spine angle throughout the backswing and then just a touch more as he reached the top. This slight downward move allowed him to turn his shoulders within the 48-inch zone.

Weight Distribution

You hear a lot of discussion about how the weight should shift from its distribution at address, up to the top of the backswing, and then down through impact. You may have heard advice that, by the top of your backswing, you should have shifted 70, 80, or even 90 percent of your weight onto your right or rear foot. Well, this may come as a surprise to you, but as a one-plane swinger you should not be trying to shift very much weight at all to your right side on the backswing. The reason: Your one-plane backswing, if properly executed, will give your swing arc plenty of width because the one-plane swing, as discussed earlier, inherently has width. Usually, when you shift your weight to the right, your legs and midsection, and possibly even your shoulders and head, will slide farther away from the target. This increases your width, which is something the one-plane swing does not lack to begin with. An exaggerated weight shift, a lateral slide to the right, and getting behind the ball are harmful for a one-plane swinger.

At the top of the backswing, your weight should be close to evenly distributed between the feet. Personally, I'd rather see you keep a little more than half your weight on your left foot as a protection against adding width. Remember, your swing arc naturally has ample width. You don't need to increase your width by moving onto your right foot as you go back. You should feel that your weight is more or less on the balls and insides of both feet, which creates stability in your lower body, the area that is the swing's structural foundation.

You might find this advice surprising, but it really shouldn't be. These days there are a number of swing measurement devices that can, among other things, measure your weight distribution at various points in the swing. A fair number of PGA Tour players have had their weight distributions measured on these devices. I think you would be surprised to find that a great many Tour pros show a weight distribution at the top of the backswing that's very close to 50-50, with some slightly favoring the left or forward foot.

If you need any further convincing about what's really right about weight distribution on the backswing, let me give you an ideal one-plane model to mimic: Ernie Els. At the top, Els keeps his weight centered beautifully.

Movement of the Club

We've now discussed all the movements your body should make in the one-plane backswing. What about the club itself? If you've moved your arms and body correctly, the club will move into the desired positions as the backswing progresses. Of course, you need to know what these club positions are and check them frequently. If you find that the club is out of place, you'll need to go through the arms and body motions so you can determine where you started to go awry.

On the takeaway, for the one-plane swing, the clubhead should *not* remain on the target line once it has started moving back. If you are turning your shoulders on plane, with your left arm snugly against the chest, the clubhead cannot stay along the target line. To keep it anywhere near the target line, you would have to push your arms out away from you, or tilt your shoulders instead of turning them, or both. So, let the clubhead move naturally to the inside.

A key checkpoint comes when the club shaft has reached hip height. At this point, the shaft should be parallel to the target line and parallel to the ground. Ask someone to stand behind you and monitor your club shaft position as it appears from directly down the target line. The club

Photos 3.6 and 3.7 **Early on in the one-plane swing, the club swings inside—automatically—as the right elbow moves up and back and the shoulders rotate clockwise.**

Photo 3.8 This is a good toe position, at this point of the swing, for a one-plane swinger.

shaft should fall over a line down to the insteps or the center of the feet. (This is quite different from the position of the two-plane player, as we'll see later.) The club shaft should also be moving on an arc or path a little closer to the body, because this swing is moving on a flatter plane and the arms have already come into the chest. Also, the clubhead's toe should point halfway between the target line and straight up, similar to the angle of your spine. This slightly closed position is necessary because the forearms have not yet begun to pronate.

If anything, I'd rather see you err toward an even more closed clubface, meaning the face would point a bit downward. It allows you to get the left arm closer to your chest even sooner. You can easily adjust the clubface direction from this point in the swing to the top by rotating your forearms more to open the face.

As the backswing continues, the plane your clubhead moves on will be somewhat wider and flatter to the ground than you may be accustomed to. Don't worry—this is what you're looking for. If you turn your shoulders along the angle you set them on at address, the club shaft will work its way behind your right shoulder and up onto the plane.

As to where the club shaft should be pointing at the top of the backswing, this is something that a lot of amateurs, and even their teachers, get tricked by. So let's clearly define our terms. At or near the top of the backswing, we want to check where the club shaft is pointing when the club is parallel to the ground. What confuses many golfers is that this particular point is very rarely the precise top of the backswing for any given player. For the majority of golfers, particularly older ones who are not extremely supple, the club shaft will never reach parallel. Then there is a large minority of top golfers, namely John Daly, who swing the club beyond parallel at the top.

This might be a good time to review that neither the length of a person's swing nor the overall speed or pace of it, are specifically tied to either a one-plane or two-plane swing. Length of swing and pace of swing are individual traits. A one-plane swing can be long or short, fast or slow. The same holds true for the two-plane swing.

At any rate, in order to compare apples to apples, we should not judge where the club shaft is pointing by the spot at which a golfer completes his or her backswing. Rather, for the golfer with the compact backswing, we must, in effect, extrapolate to make his or her swing longer, and then judge where the club shaft would be pointing if it reached a position parallel to the ground.

To most golfers who do not reach parallel at the top, it will appear that their club shaft is pointing well to the left of the target line in what is known as a "laid off" position. It may be, but the point is that if the club shaft had reached parallel, it could very well have been pointing at the target. For the player who swings beyond parallel, the problem is easier to solve. They simply need to stop the backswing at the point where the shaft reaches parallel, and then have someone observe from behind to see if it is pointing at the target. If you were to simply look at their position upon completion of the backswing, you would think the club shaft is pointing well right, in what teachers call the "cross the line" position.

That stated, at the point in the swing described, the ideal is to have the club shaft pointing parallel to your target line. For the one-plane player, however, I would like to see any error being on the side of having the club shaft pointing a little left of the target, or being a bit laid off. The reason I prefer that one-plane players be a bit laid off is that, from this position, they have the club well behind them and they can turn their torsos as hard as they like on the downswing and never swing down over the top. From a slightly laid-off position, all it really means is that the left forearm and the club will rotate a little harder back down to the correct impact position as you return your shoulders and arms back down and through the ball.

As to the position of the clubface itself, the one-plane player should have the clubface in a square position at the top, in relation to his or her swing plane. However, it's okay for the face to be slightly closed or shut in relation to your plane.

Photo 3.9 **At the top, the one-plane swinger's club should be parallel to the target line and is acceptable if it is slightly laid off.**

Let's define this square position clearly, as it's often a point of confusion. First, when checking the position of your clubface at the top, it's best to do it with a driver. This is your least-lofted club, so there is the least distortion in judging which way the clubface is pointing. A clubface that's square to your plane would be halfway between pointing to the sky and pointing perpendicular to the ground. The clubface is completely closed to your plane if it's pointing straight up to the sky. The clubface is completely open if the toe is hanging straight down, and the clubface points perpendicular to the ground. So, if you're a one-plane swinger, you want your driver's clubface to be pointing halfway between the sky and perpendicular to the ground or, if anything, angled closed so that it's pointing a bit more toward the sky. Let me explain this last point further.

I believe a square-to-closed face balances with the flatter, more rounded plane of the one-plane golf swing. That's because a shut face requires less forearm rotation in the downswing to return the clubface square at impact. All that said, if your clubface is square to your swing plane or just a little closed at the top, you're in a very desirable position to execute the one-plane downswing.

The final thought regarding the one-plane backswing concerns the sequence of movements. The arms should begin to move first. Specifically, the left arm presses into and crosses the chest while the right elbow starts up and behind you. Once the arms begin to move, the shoulders begin to turn, and then the hips. Each move follows the start of the preceding move and blends in seamlessly to the completion of the backswing.

Executing the Two-Plane Backswing

While I believe that the one-plane swing is the simplest and most technically efficient way to swing the golf club, there are plenty of two-plane swingers in the Hall of Fame. The two-plane golf swing is still considered the classic swing style, and it is certainly the type of technique that's been used the longest. In fact, if you look back at photos of golfers from the 19th and early 20th centuries, you'll notice that they wore much heavier clothing, namely, long-sleeved shirts, ties, and heavy wool jackets. No doubt if you were playing in the cool, windy weather typical of the early open courses of Scotland and England, you needed some warm clothes. However, because of the way they were bundled up, I believe they were physically unable to bend over and turn, to keep their spine angle stable, and to separate the shoulder and the hip turns in the manner that the one-plane swing requires. Therefore, they took to raising their arms above the turn of the shoulders, simply in order to move the clubhead away from the ball as far as they could. Even that was probably difficult. At any rate, what is considered the classic golf swing during the eras of Harry Vardon (1890–1910) and Bobby Jones (1920s) was most definitely the two-plane swing.

You can play wonderful golf using a two-plane swing. You can win multiple major championships, as did Tom Watson, Hale Irwin, and the late Payne Stewart. John Jacobs, who wrote the best instruction book of the modern era, *Practical Golf,* is the foremost champion of this method. In it Jacobs writes: "Should the shoulder turn match the arm-swing plane? Despite what you may have heard or read, or thought to have seen in good golfers, the answer is no. The shoulders should always turn on a more horizontal—flatter—plane than the plane of the arm-club swing."

Despite my immense respect for Jacobs, I still prefer the one-plane swing, because it does not require the degree of timing that the two-plane swing does. That said, let's look at the motions that make up the two-plane backswing, simply because your ultimate goal is to choose the best technique for you, if you haven't already.

Shoulders

The two-plane swing has an advantage in that it does not require the degree of athleticism that the one-plane swing does. Both your shoulders and your hips will be turning on virtually the same plane—there is very little winding of the shoulders against the hips.

You recall that at address, you'll be standing more erect. So naturally, when you take the club back your shoulders will make a turn that's closer to level with the ground. Thus, the plane of your shoulder turn will be well outside the ball's position and well outside that 48-inch zone outside the ball that we set for the one-plane swinger's shoulder turn.

When you make the two-plane backswing, neither the arms nor the shoulders are moving on a plane suitable for golf. The shoulder turn is on a plane that would be appropriate for a baseball batter swinging at a pitch that's chest-to-waist or hip-high in the strike zone. While that is happening, your arms will be swinging on a plane more as though you are trying to drive a tent peg into the ground. You start the backswing by turning your shoulders and torso away from the ball, as you would in a one-plane motion. However, in this swing you'll simultaneously start swinging your arms upward. You must turn your shoulders in a fairly horizontal plane while at the same time and at the same rate of speed your arms are moving upward in front of the chest. If your shoulders move around faster than your arms swing up, you'll have a very flat, wide takeaway, with the clubhead moving quickly inside the target line. As the backswing progresses, a lift action by the arms will become very evident. This inside-to-up backswing is a very prevalent move of high-handicap amateurs, and its root is in poor timing of the body parts. Less prevalent is a timing issue in which the arms swing up faster than the shoulders turn, giving you a very steep, pick-up start to the backswing. So, if your timing is off, the plane of the swing or the direction you swing along will be negatively affected. This is why timing was so important to players such as Tom Watson or Payne Stewart during their PGA Tour heydays, and the exactitude required to do this is one of the main reasons I favor developing the one-plane swing if you have the athletic ability to do so.

"As I take the club back, I try to swing slowly, keeping my arms and my body turn moving together," says PGA Tour player Duffy Waldorf.

As the backswing continues, the shoulders should continue to turn on the angle you set them on at address, with no tilting of the shoulders that would make the swing more upright. Keep turning your shoulders as far as you can, preferably at least 90 degrees from the address position. You will probably be able to turn your shoulders slightly farther in the two-plane backswing than the one-plane backswing because your hips will be turning much more.

Arms

Your arm movement in this method is, as I've said, more vertical than your shoulder turn. One thing that makes the two-plane swing distinct is that your arms swing upward while staying in front of your chest and shoulders as they turn. They actually swing in a V shape in front of your

Photos 3.10 and 3.11 These photographs clearly show how in the two-plane swing the shoulders turn on a fairly horizontal plane while the arms swing upward.

body. The point of the V represents address and impact positions. One leg of the V shows the backswing up over the right shoulder and then back down to impact. The other leg shows the follow-through swing up over the left shoulder.

Do you remember the practice exercise I mentioned for the one-plane swing, in which you put a towel or head-cover under your left arm and try to hold it there throughout the backswing and in the follow-through? Well, in a two-plane backswing you might not be able to do this. The head-cover might slip out halfway through the backswing. Still, as you make your upward arm swing, I recommend that you keep your arms relatively close to your chest. Don't let them move too far away from your body.

While your arms swing upward and stay much more in front of your body, you will not need to pronate your left forearm as you do in the one-plane backswing. In order for the arms to stay more in front of you and to gain needed width in the backswing, your right elbow may fold later. As you approach the top of the backswing, the right elbow joint of the two-plane swinger should point almost straight down to the ground. In this position the upper arm from the elbow to the shoulder should mirror the angle of the spine. It should be fairly erect to the ground. This is in contrast to the position of the elbow of the one-plane player. That player's right elbow points more to the rear and mirrors the bent-over angle of the spine. However, like the one-plane swing, if the golfer makes a mistake with the right elbow, it is far preferable to have it pointing too far behind him or her than not enough. Many great players have played with flying right elbows, but if the elbow gets moving in front of your body in either a one- or two-plane swing, the club will get stuck behind you in a position that is too flat—too much from the inside—and the face will be too open.

Another point I should mention here is the condition of your left arm as you swing to the top. In the one-plane swing, the left arm will remain straight as it swings across your chest. In the two-plane swing, with your arms slightly separating from your body and lifting upward, you'll see that it may be difficult to keep your left arm ramrod straight. If you simply cannot make a two-plane backswing while keeping your left elbow straight, it's okay to have a little bit of bend or give in it. So as you reach the top, a slightly bent left elbow, like that employed by two-time U.S. Open champion Curtis Strange in his prime, is perfectly acceptable.

If you have blended the horizontal turn of your shoulders to the upward swinging of your arms, the club should move on a steady plane up to the top. At this point, your arm swing plane should be noticeably higher than your shoulder plane when viewed from down the target line.

Hips

One of the main advantages of the two-plane swing comes in the action of the hips. In the two-plane backswing, you can turn the hips as fully as possible. Because the shoulders and hips are turning on the same plane and the major power in the swing is not coming from a windup of the upper torso against the hips, there is no need to restrict the hips in order to build tension. So, the two-plane backswing will be easier athletically to make. Still, you want to make as full a hip turn as you can, at least 45 degrees of turn from your address position. If more body turn is desired, lift the left heel in the backswing to allow your shoulders and hips to turn farther around. This is particularly good advice for golfers with limited flexibility. The two-plane swing attempts to generate power from the swinging of the arms and from the momentum of the turn by the entire body, as opposed to the winding of the upper body against the lower body in the one-plane swing.

As you reach the top, your hips should be turned at least 45 degrees from the target, preferably more. When viewed straight on, your hips should be centered over your legs or shifted a bit to the right of center. It's all right if your right leg stands more or less straight up, as opposed to it being angled in throughout the backswing as for the one-plane player. The only unacceptable position for the two-plane player is if the leg bows out. Reminder: If your hips do move a little to the right off the ball, your head should move at least a corresponding amount to the right, away from the target. Understand that I'm not advising you to consciously move your hips and head to the right. I'm just saying that a slight movement away from the target is allowable, namely because it will add a bit more width to your backswing, which is desirable because, with

Photos 3.12 and 3.13 As you can clearly see from these two photographs, the two-plane swinger's hip turn (left) is much more vigorous than that of the one-plane swinger (right).

DOUBLE-CROSS DRILL

Try this drill to see how the motion of both the torso and the hips must be wedded in the two-plane swing. On the practice range, address the ball with a six- or seven-iron, with your feet crossed, right leg in front of left leg. Go ahead and try to hit the shot with the motion of your two-plane swing. What are the results? Obviously it's more difficult to hit a ball this way. But you can see that with your feet crossed, your hips are pretty much taken out of the swing movement. Your shoulders can turn a fair amount. However, with your arms swinging in the up-and-down wood-chopping type motion I've described, your swing has very little width.

As you recall, the two-plane swing is inherently too steep and narrow. Without a full hip turn, at least 45 to 50 degrees, the swing is even narrower and steeper. This drill illustrates the absolute need for hip turn in the two-plane swing to gain width. With the hips restricted, you will notice that you will swing down very steeply into the ball rather than hitting the back of it squarely, and your swing will have very little power. While, granted, it would be hard to hit a very good shot with your feet crossed no matter what your method, you'd see better results with the one-plane swing because it does not require a full-hip turn.

your arms moving up rather than around, the two-plane backswing tends to be too narrow.

Spine Angle

As you take the club back, your spine should remain fairly erect. Take some slow practice swings in front of a mirror to make sure your spine angle doesn't drop from where you were at address. Incidentally, it's a good idea to have some masking tape handy. Putting a piece of tape on the mirror can help you check any part of your swing. In this case, you should place the piece of tape where your head was located at address. Then, as you complete the backswing, stop and see where your head is now located. If it's in the same spot, or if it's about one inch above the tape, that's fine. A little bit of rise is acceptable in the two-plane backswing. You just want to make sure you don't drop your spine, as this would make the arc of your swing steeper and narrower, which you—as a two-plane player—cannot afford. It is also acceptable if, in the backswing, your head drifts slightly to the right, behind the ball, as this will give the two-plane swing width.

If you recall, your address position for the two-plane swing called for you to cant your upper body slightly to the right in what's called an inverted K position. So at address, your spine was tilted just slightly to the right or away from the target. At the top of the backswing, it should still be tilted slightly that way, or the tilt may even be increased slightly. As mentioned, this slight movement will again add width to your backswing, providing increased speed and a more level hit.

Weight Distribution

The two-plane player will have more weight on the right foot at the top than will the one-plane player. You should be looking to shift some weight to the right, as this will contribute some width to the swing. For full shots, I would like to see you have at least 60 percent of your weight on your right foot. This may not sound like much of a difference from the 50-50 distribution that I recommended for the one-plane player, but it is significant.

Club

As you take the club away from the ball, the movement of the clubhead will be slightly different from that of the one-planer. Yes, the clubhead will move gradually inside the target line as your shoulders turn. However, because the two-plane swing is more upright than the one-plane swing, it will not move inside the target line quite as quickly as it does for the one-plane swinger. To achieve this, the arms should be beginning to lift up at the same time the shoulders begin to turn. This slight lifting action keeps the club closer to the target line. It also means that your clubhead will not stay as low to the ground as you draw it back. I'm not saying that you should consciously pick up the clubhead with a flick of your wrists. I am saying that the simultaneous lifting of the arms with the turning of the torso will raise the clubhead off the ground

Photo 3.14 As the two-plane golfer swings back, he or she should shift at least 60 percent of the weight to the rear foot. In making this shift, it's all right if the head drifts slightly to the right behind the ball as it does here.

Photo 3.15 **In taking the club back, the two-plane golfer starts it fairly straight back along the target line before moving it gradually to the inside.**

sooner. To counteract this and to keep it from rising too rapidly and thus resulting in too narrow a swing, I suggest keeping both arms fairly straight, not rigid, and extending them back away from the ball in a sweeping arc.

As you move part of the way into the backswing, again you should check the position of the club shaft as it reaches parallel to the ground, or hip height. The shaft should also be parallel to your target line. Also, when viewed from down the target line, the shaft line should be slightly outside the toes for the two-plane swinger. This is a little farther away from you than for the one-planer and results from the fact that the swing is more upright and that your arms are beginning to separate from your torso and move upward.

As the torso and hips continue to turn and the arms swing up to the top, you can see from a down-target view that the club has reached a more upright position. Specifically, it is either directly above the right shoulder or above a point between the right shoulder and the neck, as opposed to being behind and slightly higher than the right shoulder as in the one-plane swing. The club shaft is also at or above head height, as in the swing of Tom Watson, rather than at or below head height, as in the swing of Ben Hogan.

Once you reach the top, you should expect the position of both the club shaft and the clubface to be slightly different from that of the one-plane swinger. When the shaft reaches a position parallel to the ground, it should point parallel to your target line or, if anything, cross the line. The two-plane player who crosses the line a little will actually be able to drop the arms down to the inside of the backswing plane a little easier and so he or she will be able to deliver the clubhead powerfully into the ball while moving from inside to along the target line. This inside path will also shallow your downswing, which aids a solid hit. However, if you're a two-plane player, having the club laid off at the top can create some serious problems. From this laid-off position it is very difficult to get your arms and club back down to where you can swing the club in the correct direction down and through the ball. Typically, the two-plane swinger who lays the club off at the top will end up either swinging out-to-in and slicing or pulling or making a number of contortions to correct the downswing plane, usually with little success.

At the top of the two-plane swing I like to see the clubface either square to the target or slightly open. With a driver, a square clubface position would be pointing halfway between straight up toward the sky and perpendicular to the ground. Your clubface is slightly open if the toe of the driver is pointing a bit more down, so that the face points a little more perpendicular to the ground than toward the sky. I have no problem with the player's club being a little open, and you will find that when you assume a fairly weak grip as I advocated for the two-plane player, the clubface will naturally tend to be, if anything, a touch open at the top. Because the two-plane swing is on less of an arc, the hands are used more to square the clubface during impact. In a one-plane swing there is some squaring of the clubface with left-arm rotation. However, most of the clubface squaring is a result of the club being moved on a greater arc in the downswing and through impact, which squares the clubface by moving it from open-to-closed along the arc. In the two-plane swing, because it is on less of an arc, the hands and wrists roll over, or release, to square up the face. Having the clubface slightly open encourages more release and less blocking with the hands. Blocking the hands on a straight line is undesirable. More on this and the release will be addressed later in the book.

In the two-plane backswing, the arms and the shoulders are the first to move and move at exactly the same time—just before the hips start turning.

Review: One-Plane Versus Two-Plane Backswing

Once again, I realize that you have been asked to digest a great deal of information, because we have discussed in detail two very different but effective ways to develop your backswing. Therefore, to clarify any uncertainties, please review the following summary.

Photo 3.16 At the top of the swing, the two-plane golfer's club should be parallel to the target line. However, a slight across-the-line position is all right too.

The One-Plane Backswing

Shoulders: The shoulders turn on a plane such that, at the top of the backswing, a line drawn across the top of the shoulders should point within a zone between the ball and a point four feet outside or beyond the ball. The head should remain centered in the stance, and the shoulders should be turned fully, 90 degrees or more from their position at address.

WARNING
Do not let the plane of your shoulders wander toward a point more than 48 inches outside the ball, or else your backswing shoulder plane will become much too flat.

Arms: The left arm swings in and is pulled directly across the chest by the retracting right elbow moving up and back. The upper left arm stays tight to the chest. Near the top of the backswing, it turns (pronates) with the top of the forearm facing somewhat upward. The right elbow folds, moving up on a line parallel to the plane. The right arm also stays sufficiently away from the body. Both arms swing around the body, toward the rear, as opposed to remaining in front of the chest. At the top, the left arm should be very close to the same plane as the shoulders. The upper part of the right arm (from elbow to shoulder) should be at least parallel to the angle of the spine, with the right elbow pointing behind the player.

WARNING
Do not let the left arm swing above the plane of the shoulder turn.

Hips: Hips stay centered in the stance or may move slightly left during the backswing.

WARNING
Do not let the hips turn more than 45 degrees.

Spine Angle: The angle of the spine must either stay the same as at address or increase slightly (tilt the spine more downward and out). The spine stays centered over the lower body or, if anything, may tilt a bit toward the target.

WARNING
Do not allow the angle of your spine to raise up or to the right on the back-swing. This movement increases the width of the swing arc unnecessarily, flattens the shoulder turn, and decreases the tension between the shoulders and the hips.

Weight Distribution: The weight should be close to centered between the feet at the top of the backswing.

WARNING
Do not allow the majority of your weight to shift onto your rear foot. This makes the one-plane swing motion too wide and too shallow.

Club: Takeaway is to the inside. Halfway back, the club shaft is parallel to the target line and parallel to the ground and directly above a line running through the center of the feet. At the top, the club shaft should point parallel to the target line or slightly left of parallel (laid off). The shaft is slightly above and behind the point of the right shoulder. The clubface is either square to the swing plane or slightly closed (with the clubface pointing slightly more toward the sky).

WARNING
Do not let the club cross the line at the top of backswing or get the club-face into an open position at the top. Either flaw calls for substantial manipulation of the club on the downswing of a one-plane swing.

Two-Plane Backswing

Shoulders: They turn on a relatively flat plane, close to parallel to ground. At the top of the backswing, a line across the top of the shoulders should point well past the 48-inch zone beyond the ball. The head should remain centered in the stance or be shifted slightly right of center. Ideally, shoulder turn is 90 degrees or more.

WARNING
Do not tilt the shoulders.

Arms: Arms must stay in front of the torso throughout the backswing, swinging up and down in a V shape as the body turns. Arms extend away from target in the takeaway to build sufficient width into the backswing. Later, the right elbow folds so the arms may swing up and stay in front of the torso. At the top, the left arm will be on a plane line pointing to the ball, more upright than the shoulder turn. The right elbow should point somewhat vertically downward.

WARNING
Do not let the left forearm swing too far inside and around the chest. Arms must swing more vertically in front of the chest or you risk the swing plane becoming too flat.

Hips: The hips may turn an unlimited amount in the two-plane swing, more than 45 degrees is desirable. Hips stay centered in the stance at top of backswing, or the hips and head can shift slightly right of center to add width to the backswing.

WARNING
Do not attempt to limit your hip turn. This would, in turn, limit the shoulder turn because they are turning on the same plane.

Spine Angle: The spine should stay erect through the backswing, as it was at address.

WARNING
Do not increase spine angle (lean more forward) on the backswing. Doing so narrows the backswing arc.

Weight Distribution: Weight should have transferred slightly more onto the right foot at the top. Aim for a distribution of 60-40 (right side-left side) for full shots.

WARNING
Do not put weight on the left side or have it evenly balanced at the top of the backswing, as this creates an extremely narrow arc in a two-plane swing.

Club: The clubhead will stay on target line slightly longer than in the one-plane swing. When halfway back and parallel to the target and ground, the club shaft runs along a line just beyond the toe line. At the top of the backswing, the club shaft points parallel to the target line or slightly right of the target line. When viewed from behind, the club shaft is either directly above the right shoulder or above a point between the right shoulder and neck. The clubface is square to slightly open, and the toe of the club points more downward.

WARNING
Do not get the club shaft laid off at the top (pointing left of target). This makes it very difficult for the arms to drop down on the backswing without getting the downswing plane off target.

4

Get Down

Two different roadmaps for learning how to

swing the club down into the ball and make

solid clubface-to-ball contact

The downswing in golf—at least the part of the swing that starts at the top and ends at impact—only takes about one-fifth of a second. Consequently, even the most talented golfers have a difficult time bailing out a bad backswing and still returning the club squarely and solidly to the ball.

Make no mistake, the downswing is largely a reflexive action. Some players do, however, claim that they are very aware of concentrating on starting the downswing by replanting their left heel or by using a trigger involving the arms, shoulders, or hips—either rotating or clearing them in a counterclockwise direction or shifting them laterally toward the target.

I do accept that players can consciously trigger the start of the downswing action. However, I would rather have players tell me that they practiced all the vital downswing movements, using drills to groove individual actions until they became so automatic that even the trigger itself operated on automatic pilot.

One thing that can really cause a player to falter and hit a bad shot after making a technically sound backswing is bad timing, tempo, and rhythm. When the beat of the downswing is off, it negatively affects the sequencing of the body and club. This is particularly true in the case of a two-plane swinger who must depend more on the timing between the turning of the body and the sequencing of the arms to hit good golf shots.

Another thing that can disrupt the continuity of the downswing is allowing, say, a two-plane downswing fundamental to be incorporated into a one-plane action or vice versa. For example, at the start of the downswing a one-plane swinger should turn the left hip and left shoulder. However, if that same one-plane golfer triggers the downswing by shifting the hips laterally, as a two-plane golfer should do, he or she is likely to fail to return the club squarely to the ball and will hit an off-line shot as a result.

Just from this one example, I think you will understand how important it is for you to marry one-plane downswing fundamentals with one-plane backswing fundamentals and two-plane downswing fundamentals with two-plane backswing fundamentals. This is not rocket science, but it is to be taken seriously if you want to evolve as a player and hit good shots consistently.

Read the following instructions that refer to the start of the downswing, impact, and follow-through so thoroughly that you can feel the motion and clearly see it coming to life in your head. Only then will you be equipped to swing into the proper positions virtually automatically.

Executing the Start of the One-Plane Downswing

Now that you have a clear understanding of how to swing the club up to the top, whether you're using the one-plane or two-plane method, it's time to turn the one-plane downswing loose.

Shoulders

The motor or power generator in the one-plane downswing is your torso (shoulders, chest, and stomach). You must turn your shoulders (and your entire torso with them) along with your left hip to start your downswing.

Now, I am sure that a lot of you are asking yourself, "Isn't the downswing supposed to start with some movement of the lower body? Shouldn't I hold back the upper body until later in the downswing? And if I don't hold the shoulders back, won't they automatically jut outward (over the top) so that I hit a big pull or a slice?"

If this is what you are thinking, you've done a great job of remembering your previous golf lessons. Yes, you have probably heard that you should start the downswing with some form of lower-body movement, which there's no need for me to describe in detail here. But let's remember, we're making the one-plane swing here, and the parts of the one-plane swing are different from those of the two-plane swing, just as a Lexus's fuel pump is different from that of a Mercedes. And in the one-plane swing, the part that starts the downswing is your torso and your left hip. The secret is to turn the torso as hard as possible while maintaining maximum body control and balance. Incidentally, by the term torso, I mean both the upper torso (particularly the left shoulder), the middle torso (controlled by the oblique abdominal muscles), and the hips.

It's true that if you turn your shoulders rapidly at the start of a two-plane downswing you will go over the top in relation to your target line. But you don't have to worry about going over the top in the one-plane downswing (providing you execute correctly). Why won't you go over the top? Because, as you'll remember, in the one-plane golf swing the shoulders and arms are turning on the same single plane, a plane running from the top of your shoulders down to the ball or in a zone slightly outside of the ball, as described earlier. As long as your spine angle is bent over, your shoulders are turning on the correct plane well within the zone (never flat beyond the zone), and your arms and the club are

Photo 4.1 **In studying this photograph of the start of the one-plane downswing, you can see how hard the hips and shoulders are initiating the downswing. The arms are very passive.**

correctly positioned across your chest, you cannot possibly go over the top no matter how hard or how fast you turn your shoulders.

Many good players have been misled on this issue of when and how much to turn the shoulders by teachers who do not fully understand the one-plane swing concept. If you, as a one-plane swinger, are advised not to turn your shoulders, then the club, to use the popular parlance, will likely get "stuck behind you." I'll go into more detail later.

But let's get back to discussing what you *should* do. Your shoulders and torso cannot turn fast enough as long as they are turning within the zone. Incidentally, on the downswing as on the backswing, the bottom of your spine is the hot spot, so to speak, that your shoulders and torso will unwind around. You'll be releasing the pent-up tension you built on the backswing. Then, well after impact on a full swing, your torso will keep winding in the follow-through until you actually start to feel that tension in the lower spine again.

If you are doubtful that you can deliver the club from inside to inside while unwinding your shoulders rapidly, well, all I can say is look at Peter Jacobsen. Peter has said in a number of instructional interviews, "I try to turn my shoulders toward the target as fast as I can on the downswing." And Peter has obviously been able to hit the ball very straight and very powerfully, even as he makes the transition from PGA Tour player to the Champions Tour (50 and over). In 2003, at age 49, Jacobsen won the Greater Hartford Open. That is a remarkable feat given the quality of the fields on the PGA Tour.

In the one-plane downswing (as well as in the backswing) your shoulders must dominate because they need to turn much farther than your lower body does in that span of time from the top to impact, which is a mere fraction of a second. Remember, at the top of the backswing, you turn your shoulders roughly twice as much as your hips—90 degrees or more for your shoulders versus approximately 45 degrees for your hips. At impact, depending on your flexibility, your hips should be open (anywhere from 35 to 50 degrees) and somewhat facing the target. Your shoulders should be only 15 degrees or so behind the hips, with the left arm just starting to move across the chest. In other words, your shoulders have nearly caught up with the hips. To do this, your upper torso, which was wound up against the hips and lower torso, must explosively unwind faster than the hips to achieve the ideal impact position.

As you make this aggressive shoulder turn back to the ball, I want to make sure that you understand the difference between turning your shoulders and tilting them. The difference is critical. When you turn your shoulders, they revolve around your spine at a perfect 90-degree angle. I recommend that you practice making this pure turn of your shoulders—from the top of the downswing to the point of impact—in front of a full-length mirror. For now, don't give any thought to your arms, the club, or anything else. Just try to ingrain that pure turn of the shoulders and you'll also notice that the club shaft is moving along the same plane as your shoulders, at a 90-degree angle to your spine. If you simply retain the more bent-over spine angle we discussed earlier and turn your shoulders around the spine, you'll stay in the 48-inch zone and never come over the top.

The majority of amateurs (and even many professionals) do not make this pure rotation of the shoulders around the bent-over spine. Instead of turning, they tilt their shoulders from the top by dropping the right, or rear, shoulder straight down and raising the left shoulder straight up. The instant you tilt your shoulders, your spine will also rise up from its original position. How much of a problem is this? Well, it is one that even the greatest golfers in the world struggle with mightily on many occasions. Let's try a little experiment here to show you what is likely to happen when you tilt rather than turn. First, set up in a one-plane address and then take the club up to the top. From here, turn your shoulders on a plane, at right angles to your spine, until your shoulders are back to a square position. Don't do anything with your arms or the club but notice where they are. With your shoulders back to square, your arms will be about waist high and the grip end of the club shaft will be pointing at the target line. You only need to keep turning your hips and torso while your left arm rotates and naturally starts to move across your chest to deliver the club smoothly and powerfully through impact.

Next, try this. Take the club up to the top of the one-plane backswing. Instead of turning the shoulders from here, though, tilt your shoulders, so the right drops straight down and the left rises straight up. Notice how when you tilt instead of turn, your right elbow drops down to the top or in front of your hip bone. The club shaft, meanwhile, is still way behind you, the grip end pointing somewhere outside the target line. You now have the club positioned in the infamous "stuck-behind-you" position. From here, the most likely result will be that you will come through impact too much from the inside and with the club-face pointing right of target, so you'll hit well right of target. What can also happen is that you will sense that you're positioned to hit the ball to the right, so you'll make a last-instant attempt to get the clubface back to square by flipping your hands through the impact zone. Result? A quick hook.

Arms

The action of your arms in the one-plane downswing is very similar to that of a baseball swing. That is, at the top of the backswing, your left arm is across your chest with your right arm behind you, folded with the elbow pointing slightly behind you. Now, if you look at any great power hitters in baseball, you'll see that, from this position, they turn their shoulders and upper torso as hard and as fast as they can toward the coming pitch. The torso is like an inner or centripetal force whose movement activates the bat, which receives the outer or centrifugal effect. When this force and its effect are applied correctly, the bat comes through with crashing speed to meet the ball.

It's the same principle in the one-plane golf swing. You don't throw your arms and club at the ball; rather, they get thrown by the turn of the shoulders and torso. There is some rotation of the left forearm in the downswing through impact, which I will discuss shortly. But beyond that left-arm rotation, your arms (and your hands) will actually remain very passive until just before impact. The arms, until that moment, should simply stay in position, with your left arm rotating but still staying across your chest and your right arm behind the body. As your torso turns around a steady, bent-over spine, it will carry your arms, hands, and the club down along the correct plane line toward impact.

To most of you, I'm sure that the concept of not using your arms and hands actively must seem puzzling. "How will the club get back to the ball?" you ask. Well, if you turn your shoulders to dominate the downswing while keeping your spine at its original angle, your shoulder turn will be in the 48-inch zone. As a result, your arms will swiftly and surely be carried in front of you. You do not have to force them toward the ball. In fact, to do so would be a critical mistake. If your arms were to move in front of your chest as you started down, and then you turned your shoulders as hard as you could, you would indeed come over the top. Trust me on this for the moment, because we will be examining the impact position in detail shortly and everything should start coming together for you.

I want to point out here what I consider to be an erroneous instruction that was brought up in Ben Hogan's *Five Lessons: The Modern Fundamentals of Golf* regarding the arms, specifically the right elbow. Hogan's book indicated that when starting the downswing, the right elbow should lead the arm and drop downward so that it rests in front of the right hip. I guess Hogan will never know that in so saying he helped create one of the early 21st century's biggest buzz phrases in golf instruction—"getting the club stuck behind you."

Let's backtrack a minute and consider the career of a player who some would argue was the greatest shot-maker if not the greatest player in history. Great golf did not come easily to Hogan. He labored for years—even after breaking through to the winner's circle—with low ball flight and an ever-present and sometimes uncontrollable hook. Hogan was obsessed with taming it. One thing he thought would help was the above-mentioned move of dropping the elbow onto the top of the hip joint. It's clear to me that Hogan thought that by getting the right elbow in front of him he would keep the club shaft lagging behind. This, Hogan reasoned, would cause the clubface to remain well open in relation to the target line and to come into the ball from well inside the target line. I believe that Hogan originally felt that both of these factors would help him eliminate his hook. However, the more he got his clubface open on the way down, while moving on a path that was from well inside, the more he was forced to use his hands too much to flip the clubface toward square at the instant of impact. If I haven't said it already, let me state emphatically that you cannot consistently square up the clubface at impact by using independent hand action. That's true if you have a handicap of 25 or you're Ben Hogan. There's just far too much precision of movement required in too short a time.

Later in his career, however, Hogan gradually got his right arm more behind him and against his right side in the downswing, instead of so much on the front of his hip. This, in turn, placed the shaft less inside and more on plane with a much squarer clubface. I believe this to be the reason he was able to develop a downswing in which his torso turn could whip his arms and the club through impact without his having to work the clubface overly with his hands through impact.

There are a couple of terms I should clarify that relate to your arms (and the club) as you approach impact. These terms are *getting underneath the ball* and *getting on top of the ball*. Getting underneath refers to a position in which your arms and the club are approaching the impact zone on too flat a plane, usually with the clubface too open and the entire swing too much from inside the target line. This is a direct result of one or more of three mistakes. The most common mistake is tilting the right shoulder down at the start of the downswing instead of turning the shoulders. The second mistake is the one I have just mentioned, getting the right elbow too far in front of the right hip in the downswing. The third mistake is for the left arm to fail to rotate back, counterclockwise, either the right amount or at the right time to have the club on plane in the downswing. The amount the left arm rotates in the downswing is entirely dependent on your grip and the amount you rotate (pronate) it in the backswing. It is a usual rule of thumb that the stronger the grip, the less you have to rotate the left arm in the backswing and, thus, in the downswing. Conversely, the weaker the grip, the more rotation is required in both the backswing and the downswing. Therefore, whatever rotation occurs in the backswing must occur in the downswing, and it should occur throughout the downswing as the left arm is being swung down the plane by the shoulders. If you rotate the arm either insufficiently or too late, the club will be held under the plane, with the face too open and approaching the ball too much to the inside.

By contrast, when you make an on-plane shoulder turn (rather than a tilt) coming down, your arms and the club will be pulled around and down on plane as well. There should be no conscious dropping of the arms, only a rotation of the left arm. The arms just go along for the ride as the shoulders turn on plane. The overall sense of how your arms work in the one-plane swing is that they are constantly rotating and revolving around the body. However, because your upper body is bent over, the arms, as they move around the torso, are moving up and down and then back up a plane line. If you are a golfer who has been used to making a conscious downward movement with your arms in relation to your body, this passive arm element will make the downswing feel as though you're coming over the top. What you are actually doing is getting the clubhead more out and on top of the ball—that is, the clubhead is a little more off the ground and much closer to the target line as it enters the impact zone.

Hips

If you've heard or read a great deal of golf instruction, you might expect to hear about what your hips should be doing in great detail here. Actually, that's not the case in the one-plane downswing. Remember, your torso is the motor of your downswing. The hips do turn but are not the main engine. If you recall, your hips should have turned only half as much as your torso on the backswing. So they have only half as far to return on the downswing in the same amount of time that the torso makes its much larger downswing turn. If too much focus is placed on the hips, they can easily overpower the shoulders, resulting in the swing being thrown off-plane. Having said that, the hips do have one important move to make, one that serves to trigger the entire downswing movement. As your torso just reaches its position at the top, or even the slightest fraction before the backswing is completed, start turning your left hip back to the left.

Think of the swing movement in terms of counting to three. Ordinarily, you'd think of the swing as a one-two movement—that is, you'd count "one" for the backswing and "two" for the downswing. In the one-plane swing, you should think of the swing as having three parts: "One" for the backswing, then "two" as you set weight onto your left foot and slightly begin to turn the left hip back to the left, and "three" as you turn your upper body and hips as quickly as possible back down to the ball.

You may ask, "Why must I start the left hip during 'two,' a fraction before I complete the backswing turn?" Here's the important reason why: If you recall, in the one-plane backswing, your shoulders and upper back are turning on a far more bent over, vertical plane than the hips. As you reach the top, you're building tremendous torque between the upper body and the hips. When you start turning your left hip even slightly to the left as your backswing turn is reaching its completion, you increase the tension to such a degree that your torso just has to snap back. The hip turn is thus the trigger for your left shoulder to begin the downswing. This small, almost imperceptible move is evident in the baseball swing as well as the golf swing. Ted Williams, still considered by many the best hitter ever, said that he shifted his right hip toward the pitcher (Williams was a left-handed hitter) while still turning away from the pitcher a fraction of a second *before* his shoulder and arms took his bat all the way back. In this way, Williams triggered the release of the pent-up energy in his torso for a full, free cut at the ball. It's the same thing in the golf swing.

Many golfers might argue that they have heard that they should have a pronounced pause at the top of the backswing. A pause is great for a two-plane swing, but does not belong in a one-plane swing. The reason is a one-plane swing has a more constant loading and unloading of body torque. I can assure you that any player who exhibits a noticeable pause at the top of his or her backswing is not utilizing one of the key principles of the one-plane swing—namely, to employ an on-plane, full turn of your shoulders against the more horizontal, much lesser turn of the hips. If you do this, and then make that slight turn of the left hip just as your shoulders get to the top, you can let your shoulders turn and rotate through the ball to the finish. In short, you won't be able to pause.

I can think of no better illustration of this than Ben Hogan. There are some purists who have criticized Hogan's swing on the grounds that his tempo was quick, with no leisurely pause at the top, and was therefore not as aesthetically pleasing as some others'. But Hogan stored and then released tremendous energy during his backswing-to-downswing transition. I urge you to strive to do the same by using the slight turn of your left hip to release your stored-up energy. Let others worry about their pause at the top.

Other than this slight turning of the left hip during the transition and the rotation of the shoulders during the downswing, there's really not much else you need to concentrate on. As the downswing hurtles toward and then past impact, the hips will continue to turn but only in response to the powerful in-the-zone turning of your torso and at a much slower rate.

Spine Angle

Ideally, keep your spine bent forward during the downswing at the same fairly steep angle (approximately 35 to 45 degrees) that you started with at address. Remember that it's okay for the one-plane swinger to increase the angle slightly during the swing, to bend slightly more toward the ball. This allows you to make an even steeper shoulder turn. But you must make certain that you never rise up out of your posture—that is, lift your spine. Doing so in the downswing flattens your shoulder turn and puts your shoulder above and in front of the correct plane. Once this happens, you'll be forced to make any number of last-ditch corrections to get the clubface squarely through the ball. Unfortunately, these seldom work.

When viewed from a face-on perspective, your spine should remain as close to centered as possible, as opposed to the two-plane swinger's inverted K position, which causes the spine to lean back to the right.

Weight Distribution

When you turn your left hip just an instant before the start of the downswing, between 50 and 60 percent of your weight should be shifted onto your forward foot. As stated above, this must happen in the "two" or transition period before the downswing begins, not during the downswing.

A problem I see with many amateurs is that they make a big lateral slide to the left with their hips and legs on the downswing. They seem to think that nearly all their body weight has to get onto their left side. This isn't true. That big lateral slide is very helpful for the two-plane swing, as I shall point out shortly, but it is disastrous for the one-plane. It takes the club off its turning arc and puts it on too straight a line for a one-plane swing. The results are usually pushes and hooks. It is also very hard on the back, as it forces you into the "Reverse C" position that was in vogue some 30 years ago. So avoid any hard, jolting moves onto the left side in an attempt to transfer more weight than you need to.

Less often I'll see amateurs who make a sort of backing-up move with their hips, in which the hips sway to the right as their arms are thrown outward into the downswing. Usually it is higher handicappers who make this move, which puts the majority of their weight on their right foot as they come down. Backing-up the hips also tends to straighten the spine angle and throw the right shoulder outward or toward the ball. Now we really do have that coming-over-the-top move that all golfers fear. Remember to make that slight turn of your hips to the left to get the downswing started. The key is not to make a big move but rather to make this small move early. Shifting your weight to the left before the downswing starts has the effect of pulling in the arc of the swing slightly, again making the angle of attack sharper, as is the goal of the one-plane player.

Club

The fashionable fault in golf today, if there is such a thing, is getting the club stuck behind your body as you approach the ball from too far inside the target line with the clubface open. Many golfers have feared this will happen in the one-plane downswing, particularly in light of the fact that you are doing very little with your hands and arms. The implication is that if you don't do something with the arms they will fall way behind. Let me reiterate: If you execute the one-plane downswing correctly, you are never going to get the club stuck behind you. If you turn your shoulders on plane, actively and correctly, and rotate your left arm correctly, the club will be carried out and around on the correct plane toward the ball. You do not need to be concerned about where the club is. Just keep turning your shoulders on plane while holding the right elbow behind you and rotating your left forearm and the club will take care of itself.

Executing the Start of the Two-Plane Downswing

I have pointed out a number of outstanding players who have utilized the two-plane golf swing during their golf career. While it is possible to be a Hall of Fame player this way, as I have said earlier, I believe it is a very difficult task to consistently hit the ball both long and straight with a two-plane swing. It is not that difficult to hit the ball a long way with a two-plane swing because there are multiple sources for the generation of power. However, even tiny mistakes in the timing of the more individualized movements of the arms or the body can certainly affect the

Photos 4.2 and 4.3 Studying these two pre-impact photographs of the two-plane downswing will help you learn and visualize the proper movements, involving those for the shoulders, arms, hips, and golf club.

plane of your swing. Thus, I think it's much harder to consistently hit the ball straight with a two-plane swing.

Some two-plane swingers who were very long hitters gradually learned how to sacrifice a little bit of their power in order to keep the timing between the body and the arms synchronized. I mentioned that one of the best modern-day examples was the late Payne Stewart. He learned how to time his swing motion over the years, developing the beautifully flowing style that made him much more accurate while still providing more than acceptable distance. Stewart won three major championships and was an immense talent, but I believe he, along with Tom Watson and Davis Love III, are exceptional in what they have accomplished with the two-plane swing.

We have seen how the two-plane swing's tendency is too narrow and too steep. I have discussed several elements in the address position and in the backswing that aid in promoting width. At address, the inverted

K position and putting slightly more weight on the right leg are both widening positions. In the backswing, I have mentioned two moves that gain width: Moving your head and upper torso to the right and sweeping your arms well back away from the target. The downswing has some width-adding moves as well, and those will be discussed soon. That said, let's look at what goes into the two-plane downswing.

Shoulders

As opposed to what I stressed for the one-planer, at the start of the two-plane downswing you must keep your shoulders as passive as possible. You must avoid making any conscious turning move with the shoulders, even though this is somewhat of a natural instinct. Even worse would be any tilting of the shoulders, with the right shoulder dipping straight down and the left moving straight up, as we discussed in the one-plane swing. But your shoulders are not the motor in the two-plane swing. Your arms are the motor. Therefore, keep your shoulders quiet and their movement will follow the other body parts, as I'll describe.

Arms

The biggest difference in the two-plane downswing is that your arms must separate themselves from your torso to start the downswing. Whereas the arms move around the chest in the one-plane swing, the sensation of the two-plane swinger is that the arms move down and up in a very steep fashion, like the shape of the letter V. On the downswing, your arms form the downward leg of the V and then form the upward movement on the other side of impact.

At the top of the two-plane backswing, the hands are above the right shoulder. When you make this downward movement of the arms, you drastically widen the angle that was formed by your hands and your shoulders, with the right elbow as the other point of the triangle. It is almost as if you were making a karate chop at a board by your right side at about hip height. This downward chop of the arms is the prime power source for the two-plane downswing. Remember, you must drive your arms straight down your right side. Many golfers think they should swing their arms and the club at the ball. Wrong! If you swing your arms at the ball you will be swinging your arms too much out and not enough down on the inside.

The result will be a steep out-to-in chop at the ball. If there is a secret to the two-plane swing, it is the downward separation of the arms toward your right side rather than at the ball that allows you to hit from the inside.

At the same time that your arms start driving down in front of the right side of your chest, you must simultaneously start to turn your entire torso, from the shoulders through the hips, counterclockwise or to the left. The turning of your torso is nearly horizontal, at right angles to your spine, which as you recall is tilted forward only slightly. The key to success in the two-plane swing is keeping these two gears meshed correctly. One move cannot be sooner or faster or more pronounced than the other.

Let's touch on the most common errors that occur with regard to the arm movement during the downswing. The first is when players do not separate their hands from their shoulders fast enough—that is, they don't widen the angle as I described already. If they do not adequately drive the arms and club downward, where will the clubhead be when they turn the torso through the shot? The answer is that the clubhead will be outside the target line or over the top well before impact. This is probably the more common error. Conversely, a large minority of golfers will drive their arms down before they make the body turn. When this happens, they'll have a downswing that is much too shallow and in-to-out. Fat and thin shots are the most common result, as well as pushes and hooks.

There's an interesting width-adding addendum to the two-plane, start-down arm swing. Among top players with the two-plane method, there are a fair number who actually uncock their wrists just slightly, so that the clubhead moves farther away from the target as they begin the downswing. This is the infamous move known as "casting" the clubhead. But it is not all bad for the two-plane swinger to cast just a bit from the top. This unorthodox cast action widens your swing arc and gives you an extra instant to turn and keep the body synchronized with the arms. Furthermore, by getting the clubhead a little farther behind the body, it allows you to turn your body through the shot more without getting steep, which increases power. Three excellent examples of this slight casting move are Tom Watson on the Champions Tour and David Toms and K. J. Choi on the PGA Tour, all outstanding two-plane swingers of the golf club.

Having cited the cast action, I want you to realize that there are other measures that can be taken by two-plane swingers to widen their swing arc. My personal favorites are the inverted K position at address, sweeping the arms in the backswing, and the aforementioned slight early uncocking of the wrists on the downswing. My least favorites are the head move to the right in the backswing and the Reverse C position in the downswing. Excessive head movement makes the two-plane swinger even more dependent on timing, while the Reverse C position causes back problems.

Hips

The downswing begins with a slight lateral shift of the hips toward the target. A split second later, and simultaneous with the downward drive of the arms, your hips start turning in a horizontal fashion. Your left hip begins to turn to the left and the right hip turns outward, toward the ball. This is not a difficult move to make; the trick is in timing the move correctly

"When I was a two-planer, I felt that I started my downswing by sliding my left hip toward the target and dropping my arms into the slot," says Champions Tour player Peter Jacobsen. "I also felt like I kept my back to the target while swinging my arms down."

The tendency among the majority of amateurs, as I mentioned earlier, is to turn the shoulders and hips faster than they drive the arms downward. But the moves can be mistimed either way. The best way to tell how well you are timing the two moves is to work on it out on the practice tee while hitting a five-iron. I suggest a five-iron because it is a club with which you should have an angle of attack that is of medium steepness. You want to strike a somewhat descending blow so that you catch the ball first, without getting grass between the clubface and the ball. If you're turning your shoulders and hips too quickly, your arms will usually stay too high for too long, which will cause you to swing the club into the ball very steeply. Conversely, if you drive your arms down to the right side faster than you turn your shoulders and hips, you'll tend to come from too far inside the target line with a shallow angle and hit some type of bad shot, such as a fat, thin, push, or hook. Keep working on your timing with the five-iron; a crisp impact and a rising ball flight will give you the feedback that you're right on.

One thing you may notice among some very fine two-plane swingers, such as Tom Watson, is that they often have a noticeable amount of lateral movement of the legs toward the target at the start of the downswing. This use of the legs serves the purpose of slowing down the torso turn slightly, and this can be helpful to the overall timing of the body to the arms. However, I would rather see you work on timing the two movements rather than adding the legs into the timing equation.

Spine Angle

When viewed from down-target, the two-plane player should strive to keep his or her spine at the same angle it was at address, tipped down just a bit from vertical. If the two-plane swinger lifts this spine angle slightly, it is not nearly as significant an error as it is for the one-plane swinger. However, any noticeable lowering of the spine angle will narrow and steepen the swing arc, reducing power as well as making consistent club-to-ball contact less likely. So strive to keep the spine angle constant. A good way to check on this is to have a friend hold a yardstick lightly on top of your head from behind you as you swing. There should be very little space between the yardstick and your head as you swing down to impact.

Weight Distribution

I mentioned that the hips shift the weight slightly toward the left side as the first move of the downswing. However, let me stress that this is a *slight* transfer of the weight—it should move from 60 percent on the right or rear foot at the top of the backswing to no more than 60 percent on the left leg during the downswing. In other words, at most, 20 percent of your weight should shift from one foot to the other during the two-plane swing. Most golfers think they must shift their body weight to the right on the backswing and to the left on the downswing to a much greater extent than this. Not so. Doing so leads to a host of other faults, of which tilting and swaying the entire body are prime examples. So just make that almost-imperceptible shift of the hips toward the target as the first move down, and let your weight distribution take care of itself from there.

Club

The downward movement of the golf club should be governed by an arms-controlled swinging motion. You do not need to consciously guide the club through the downswing. What will happen is that, immediately as you start widening that angle between the hands and your right shoulder, the clubhead will start to be carried downward. If you blend this movement together with the horizontal turn of your torso, then the clubhead will begin to describe a downswing arc that is on plane with your extended left arm.

For the vast majority of golfers, you should not try to manipulate the club in any way as you start down. You may recall that I did mention three top players (Watson, Toms, and Choi) who do slightly uncock their wrists just a fraction as the downswing commences, thus increasing the width of their arcs. While such a move is acceptable, it must be slight and never fast or violent. If you are a two-plane swinger and you try to increase the amount of wrist cock on the downswing, you will likely draw the clubhead in a bit tighter to you. This downcock action is a narrowing move and thus one you definitely don't want incorporated into your downswing—particularly if you are a two-plane player.

Review: One-Plane Versus Two-Plane Start-Down Keys

The start of the downswing is a critical segment of the golf swing. You must make the right start-down move depending on your type of swing, because it is extremely difficult to correct your mistakes once you're into the downswing. In order to be certain you are clear about what to do to get either the one-plane or the two-plane downswing started correctly, a summary of the above discussion follows.

Start of the One-Plane Downswing

Shoulders: Your shoulders and upper torso should begin to unwind immediately on the same plane or on a slightly steeper plane they turned along on the backswing. It is best to key in on the left shoulder turning up and to the left. The turn of the shoulders must be the dominant move starting the downswing, because the shoulders were coiled much more than the hips and thus have the farthest to travel. Keep the shoulders turning at right angles to your spine.

> **WARNING**
>
> Do not tilt the shoulders at the start of the downswing. Tilting the right shoulder straight downward or the left shoulder straight upward leaves the club stuck behind the right side of your body, which will make the club off plane. Also, tilting instead of turning robs power from your main power source.

Arms: The arms must remain as passive as possible at the start of the one-plane downswing. The left arm remains in position across and against the chest. It rotates counterclockwise as the shoulders and upper torso turn around the spine. The right arm remains in its folded and back position, with the elbow on your right side and not in front of it. As the torso turns, it carries the arms down along the desired plane line.

> **WARNING**
>
> Do not make any active movement with your arms other than the rotation of the left forearm during the downswing. Your arms and the club will be whipped down and through the ball in response to the turning force of the shoulders and upper torso. Swinging the arms away from the chest at the start of the downswing will push the club outside the target line—"over the top."

Hips: The hips should ideally begin to turn to the left an instant before the downswing begins. This move in effect triggers the downswing movement of the upper body. This very slight hip movement is the "two" movement in the one-two-three count of the swing (backswing, transition hip move, downswing).

> **WARNING**
>
> Do not try to pause before starting the downswing. While not in and of itself a problem, a pause is an indicator that you have not coiled your upper body sufficiently against the base of your spine, which in turn means that your downswing will lack explosive power.

Spine Angle: The spine should ideally stay tilted forward from the waist at the same angle (about 35 to 45 degrees) as you started with at address. A slight increase in the angle on the downswing is not a flaw for the one-plane swinger. When viewed from the front, the spine should remain centered over the hips.

WARNING
Do not raise the spine angle at any point in the one-plane swing. Raising the spine angle puts the shoulders flat and off plane and forces the arms to separate downward from the body in an effort to hit the ball.

Weight Distribution: Weight should be distributed evenly between the two feet or *slightly* favor the left or forward leg. The left foot should be flat on the ground as the downswing commences.

WARNING
Do not make an excessive lateral slide toward the target, with a major shifting of weight onto the left foot. Doing so puts the club's downward arc too much on a straight line, defeating the rotary in-to-in benefits of a one-plane swing.

Club: The club remains passive as the downswing starts. Essentially, it will be carried to impact by the rotation of the left arm and by the turning of the torso along the desired plane line.

WARNING
Don't try to manipulate the club with your hands as you start down.

Start of the Two-Plane Downswing

Shoulders: The shoulders must remain as passive as possible at the start of the two-plane downswing. They should avoid excessive turning and should never tilt (rear shoulder moving straight down, forward shoulder straight up).

WARNING

Do not actively turn the shoulders independently of the hips. The turn of the shoulders will blend with the movements of the arms and the torso, not lead them.

Arms: The arms are the motor of the two-plane downswing. They immediately separate from the shoulders (widening the angle and the distance between hands and shoulders), driving the clubhead downward in a nearly vertical motion.

WARNING

Do not be passive with your arms.

Hips: The left hip begins the downswing with a lateral shift to the left. As the arms swing down, the hips begin to turn to the left, with the right hip beginning to turn outward. This horizontal turn of the hips must be timed with the downward driving of the arms in order to move the club down on the slightly steeper plane of the two-plane swing motion.

WARNING

Do not turn the hips too quickly. The tendency is to move them faster than the downward driving of the arms, so that, again, the arms and club go over the top.

Spine Angle: The spine should be the same as it was at address and on the backswing, bent forward only slightly. From a face-on view, the spine should be slightly canted to the player's right.

WARNING

Do not increase the spine angle on the downswing (i.e., bend more from the waist). Doing so narrows the swing arc and leads to poor contact, most often fat shots.

Weight Distribution: The downswing actually begins with a slight lateral shift of the hips toward the target, just before they begin turning horizontally. This in effect is a very minor rebalancing from the backswing to the downswing. As you swing down toward impact, about 60 percent of your weight should be on your left foot.

WARNING

Do not shift too much weight to the left. While more weight is transferred from the right foot to the left in the two-plane downswing, it is still a subtle transfer of about 20 percent of the total body weight. Your weight should never shift onto the outside of your left or forward foot.

Club: The club is pulled downward vertically by the arms. There should be no independent hand action. The only exception is that it is allowable for the wrists to uncock just slightly as you start down. This move widens your swing arc and allows your body to turn more through the shot, adding power.

WARNING

Do not guide the club down and through impact. You must trust the timing of the key movements of the two-plane downswing to move the clubhead on a correct and consistent plane down and through the ball.

The Moment of Truth: Impact!

The consistent, square delivery of the clubface to the ball is the goal of everything we have talked about so far. If you can consistently deliver the clubface squarely to the back of the ball, whether it be by employing the one-plane or the two-plane swing method, you are going to play good golf. No, you are not likely to strike the ball as well as Peter Jacobsen, Paul Azinger, Duffy Waldorf, Scott McCarron, or other PGA Tour players I work with. To expect to get the same results as they do is unrealistic if you are a weekend player.

That said, though, once you start to deliver the club squarely and solidly to the back of the ball, you may be amazed at the quality of the shots you are able to hit. The ball will seem as if it is jumping off the clubface at a much greater velocity. You'll notice that the shot's flight seems stronger—the ball bores through most any wind rather than being tossed off-line by even a moderate breeze. Furthermore, if you keep working on the mechanics we discussed so that you keep striking the ball squarely and solidly for an extended period of time, you'll not only find the game physically easier but much less taxing mentally as well. You'll get to where you can step on the tee of a hole at your home course that has always given you trouble and carry with you a completely different outlook.

Say this hole has out-of-bounds that's well to the left and trees to the right, although the fairway itself is actually quite wide. At some point in the past, you pulled or hooked a few tee shots out of bounds on this hole. Being an intelligent golfer, you knew that this was a costly mistake that you didn't want to repeat again. However, in the past, you could rarely predict where your shots would fly, because you were not in the habit of consistently hitting the ball solidly. So you began to aim well right on this hole and put a defensive swing on the ball. Result? You almost always hit it in the trees on the right or you overworked your hands to compensate for the aim to the right and hit the hook to the left that you were trying to avoid in the first place.

However, once you have begun swinging the club on the correct plane and hitting the ball solidly, you'll be able to predict the flight and the line of your shots. Now when you step onto this particular tee, do you know what will happen? The out-of-bounds stakes 20 yards left of the fairway are not going to strike fear into you. Neither will the trees. You'll say to yourself, "That fairway is 40 yards wide, and there's about 70 yards between those out-of-bounds stakes left and the trees right. There's no way I'll hit into either of them." And you won't.

If this scenario excites you, I think it would be wise for us to review the positions the body and the club should be in at the instant the club-face meets the ball. My purpose here is not to tell you how to adjust yourself at impact. As I've pointed out a number of times, the downswing happens too quickly for you to make any specific adjustments of the body or the club (even if you could sense the need for them). I think you'll find it instructive to see and know what your impact position should look like, just as you should be able to see the correct address position or various other positions during the swing. It will certainly help you to rehearse these positions in front of a mirror. The more different they feel from the manner that you're accustomed to setting up and swinging, the more I recommend mimicking these static positions. When you get out on the practice tee, you'll be working to develop a smooth motion in which your body flows smoothly through the various positions from address to follow-through. But you must understand how the static positions look and feel before you will be able to ingrain them into your new golf swing.

Impact Positions for the One-Plane Swing

Shoulders

Have you ever viewed a stop-action photo of a baseball player at the moment of impact with the ball? When viewed from the perspective of the pitcher, you'll notice that the hitter's shoulders and chest have turned well beyond their position prior to when the pitch was delivered. His torso is facing the pitcher. At the same instant his arms and the bat are extended over the plate. This is his impact position with the baseball.

Photos 4.4–4.6 Just look how free and powerful this one-plane swing is in the impact and follow-through areas!

With the exception of the bent over spine and the more vertical shoulder turn, the position of your shoulders and chest are somewhat similar to this for the one-plane impact position. They should be open by at least 30 degrees in relation to the target line, which is a technical point that surprises many amateur golfers. They think the shoulders should be square in relation to the target line, as they were at address. Not so. Your shoulder turn is the primary source of power in the one-plane downswing. The shoulders must turn as fast as they can, and they must turn beyond their original address position at impact. They are in effect cracking the whip, with the whip being your arms and the golf club. Your arms and club will feel at impact as though they are being slung or flailed from impact on into the follow-through. To feel this, make some baseball swings at an imaginary ball that is waist or chest high. Turn your torso until it faces between the pitcher and third baseman before you allow your arms to fling across your chest. The farther and faster around you can turn your chest, the more power you can generate. You are now imitating a pull hitter in baseball. You can easily feel the difference in power between this method and a push or opposite-field hitter, who uses very little torso rotation but relies instead on an early arm swing. The pull hitter hits for power; the opposite-field hitter hits singles.

A final note about the shoulders: At impact and just beyond, the shoulders, if turning in the zone, will reach their steepest point here. The left shoulder will be at its highest point, and a line down through the right shoulder will be in its most vertical position.

Arms

Your arms are somewhat opposite the right side of your torso as you enter the impact area. This is because most of the torso has already turned past being square to the target line and now is in an open position in relation to the target line. Your left or lead arm should be virtually straight and should be rotating and starting to move across the chest. As for your right arm, it is in the process of unbending from its position at the start of the downswing and is beginning to release into the follow-through. However, it should still be slightly bent as you reach impact. (If your right arm were to completely extend prior to impact, you would have used your arms too early and you'd almost certainly stick the club-head into the ground or pop up out of your spine to avoid the ground.)

As we talked about on the downswing, you also want to make sure your right elbow is almost touching but just behind the right hip, rather than getting in front of the right hip. Having the elbow just behind the right hip indicates that the clubhead has entered the hitting zone more on top of the ball than on the inside. Again, when you come into impact on top of the ball, your swing and your club are on plane and there is no need for any type of manipulation in order to make square contact.

Also at impact, the back of the left forearm and the back of the left hand are pointing at the target. The wrists and hands should be just slightly bowed backward. As discussed earlier, the amount of left-arm rotation actually depends to a great extent on the grip you employ. The stronger the grip, the less you will rotate (supinate) the left arm through impact. (You may recall that I recommended that the one-plane player employ a grip that is, if anything, leaning toward the strong position.) And as your left forearm rotates, the tendency will be for the left wrist to bow back slightly. Despite what you may have read or heard elsewhere about the left wrist leading at impact, this is perfectly acceptable and in keeping with the positions and movements of the entire one-plane swing. Finally, your wrists should be fully uncocked at impact. This uncocking will happen naturally as your arms are whipped around and down by the force of your torso turning. Do not attempt to consciously uncock the wrist at any particular point in the downswing.

A final note here about how the arms and torso work together at impact that just might be the secret to the one-plane swing. In the one-plane swing downswing, your arms are across your chest and opposite your right side. As a result, when your torso is nearing impact, it is fac-ing into the start of the follow-through portion of the plane while the arms are behind, still facing the end of the downswing portion of the plane. It is at this point that your arms start being whipped across your torso—from the right side to around the left side. Although the left arm should continue to rotate to the end of the swing, just before impact, the right arm begins to straighten and roll over the left arm. This release of the right arm over the left arm starts to be completed during the follow-through. However, it must be initiated before impact. If the right arm release is late, the arm will fail to swing around the chest correctly and the in-to-in element of the one-plane swing will be destroyed. This left arm rotating and the right arm releasing over the left arm is very dynamic. It transfers the power from the turning torso into a whipping golf club. It is the difference in baseball between a check swing and a home run. In golf, it is the difference between a weak drive in the rough and a 300 yarder in the fairway. I cannot overstate the importance of the left arm rotation and release of the right arm. A one-plane swinger can release the arms as hard as desired as long as the club is moving in an arc. The clubhead must be moving left, back to the inside immediately after impact. Problems occur when a one-planer releases on a straight line.

The faster and harder your torso can turn left and up the plane, the harder and faster you can simultaneously rotate the left arm and release the right arm. The result is a swing that is tearing through impact, producing powerfully hit straight shots.

Hips

The hips, although they have not turned as fast as the shoulders, have continued to turn. At impact, they are open by anywhere from 35 to 50 degrees or even more in relation to the target line. The amount depends on the golfer's flexibility, strength, and ability to keep the left arm across the chest and the hands somewhat opposite the right side of the torso. The hips will be turned open by about 15 degrees more than the shoulders at the point of impact. Remember, the hips did not turn nearly as much as the shoulders on the backswing. Therefore, the hips will be ahead of the shoulders all the way through the downswing. By impact, the shoulder turn has almost but not quite caught up to the turn of the hips. Also, the hips should be tilted just enough to accommodate the fairly steep shoulders turning around the spine.

Spine Angle

The spine should be set at the same angle of forward lean as at address. Because it is acceptable for the one-plane swinger to increase the spine angle at the start of the downswing, the angle may decrease (i.e., the spine rises slightly) at impact. One difference in the spine of the one-plane swinger at impact is that there may be a slight tilt of the spine to the player's right. You shouldn't consciously lean to the right, of course. But what happens is that when you turn your shoulders on a steeper angle through the impact zone as the one-planer does, your head will tend to drop back just slightly to the right. The spine will also tilt slightly right to support the head.

Weight Distribution

The one-plane swinger exhibits a very stable weight distribution at impact. The weight should be just about evenly distributed between the two feet, with no more than 60 percent on the left leg. The left foot is flat on the ground, with the weight that is on that leg never going to the outside of that foot. The right foot is not necessarily flat to the ground, nor should it be completely up on the right toes. It is somewhere between the two positions. The weight distribution is indicative of the role of the legs as stabilizers in the one-plane swing, while the upper-body turn is the chief power producer.

Club

Of course, if you have executed correctly, the clubhead should be delivered square to the target line at impact. It is delivered from just slightly inside the target line (rather than from well inside) and will be moving to the left or inside the target line immediately after impact. This in-to-in arc is crucial to the one-plane swing.

At impact, the club shaft is positioned a bit differently than it was at address. First, the shaft is leaning slightly toward the target as opposed to pointing straight up and down. This is because the hands, arms, and club are still in the process of catching up to the shoulder turn, with the clubhead being the end of the whip, slightly trailing the hands. Meanwhile, the club shaft is also more upright than it was at address. This tends to occur in the one-plane swing. At impact the shoulders have turned past where they were at address, and the left shoulder is much higher. This higher left shoulder lifts the handle of the club slightly from where it was at address, resulting in a more upright shaft at impact. What this also means, in essence, is that your wrists are more fully uncocked than they were at address. Thus your hands are slightly higher, your wrists are more arched, and the club shaft is pointing slightly more vertically downward in the one-plane impact position than it was at address.

Impact Positions for the Two-Plane Swing

Shoulders

You will notice that there are some very visible differences between the impact positions of the one-plane and the two-plane player. Because the two-plane player's arms are more active and are not lagging the body turn, it stands to reason that the body will not be turned so much ahead of the arms and the club.

The two-plane player's impact position should much more closely mimic the address position. You should feel as though you are keeping the shoulders closed to the target line for as long as possible on the downswing while your mid/lower torso is turning and your arms drive the club

Photos 4.7–4.8 **Mentally rehearse these classic impact and post-impact two-plane swing positions and you'll be more apt to employ them physically.**

downward. Therefore, at impact, your shoulders should be either square to the target line or just slightly open.

If you happen to be one of those two-plane players who casts the club slightly from the top of the backswing, then at impact your shoulders (as well as your hips) should be slightly more open to the target line. With the clubhead a little wider and farther behind you early in the downswing, you can and will need to turn your body a little more actively to get the clubface squarely through the ball. However, in all likelihood, your shoulders would still not be open to the degree that a one-planer's would be.

Arms

The arms will have swung down and should be directly in front of your body, in a position that is very similar to the inverted K of the address position. Your left arm will be straight while the right arm is just slightly bent (the right arm will be fully straightened when the clubhead is just two feet beyond impact). Your wrists should be fully uncocked, which brings the clubhead down to ball level while adding speed to the clubhead. Your left arm may be rotated (supinated) somewhat toward the target. The degree of supination is related to your grip: If you have a fairly weak grip, the arm will be supinated more so that the back of the forearm and wrist are facing the target. If your grip is stronger, there will be less supination so the back of the forearm faces slightly upward. For the player with more supination of the left forearm, there may be a slight bowing of the back of the left wrist away from the target.

"I try and return to impact as close to address as I can," says PGA Tour player Duffy Waldorf. "If I'm trying to hit a hook shot, I feel my arms and the club get to impact slightly before my body. For a fade, I picture the shoulders beating the arms and the club back to the ball."

Hips

The two-plane swinger's hips will also more closely resemble where they were at the address position than the one-plane swinger's. Again, this is because the body turn is being coordinated with the arm swing rather than the body being the leader and pulling the arms and the club through the ball. Therefore, two-plane player's hips should be either square to the target line or slightly open at impact.

When viewed from face-on, the player's right hip should be just slightly lower than the left or lead hip, as it was in the inverted K position at address.

Spine Angle

The spine angle at impact, when viewed from down the target line, should be fairly erect as it was at address, which is to say bent forward no more than 20 degrees. If you have raised the spine angle at all during the backswing, as some good two-plane players do, adding to the width of the swing arc, then the spine angle must be lowered commensurately in the downswing so that you are at the correct level at impact. Let me repeat that any raising or lowering of the spine angle during the swing is best kept to a minimum, as it adds to timing problems.

The two-plane player's spine when viewed face-on has been tilted just slightly to the right since address. At impact, it is acceptable to slightly increase this spine tilt to the right. A bit more tilt to the right tends to widen or flatten out the bottom part of the swing arc, which is especially desirable for the two-plane swinger. The longer flat spot ensures a flush hit of clubface on ball, which imparts the greatest possible energy to the shot.

Weight Distribution

As opposed to the minimal weight shifting of a one-plane player, a two-planer makes a more active transfer in two directions. On the backswing, a two-plane swinger transfers a fair amount of weight onto the inside of the right leg. Then at the start of the downswing, the player shifts weight to the left, so that the majority of it (about 60 percent) is on the left leg. This amount should remain on the left side through impact. Although a lateral weight shift to the left has occurred, remember that the upper body should still be behind the ball in the inverted K position, with the arms in front and the shoulders remaining passive.

Club

At impact, the clubface should be square to the target line. The club shaft is in a very similar position to where it started at address. Unlike the one-plane player whose club shaft may be more upright than at address, the two-planer's shaft angle should be the same. That's because the two-plane player's body at impact closely mirrors the address position and has not turned as actively as the one-planer's must.

Review: One-Plane Versus Two-Plane Impact Positions

One-Plane Impact

Shoulders: The shoulders are turned along the same tilted plane as throughout the swing. Shoulders are open by at least 20 to 30 degrees in relation to the target line. Just beyond impact the shoulders will be in their steepest position.

WARNING
Do not try to keep your shoulders square to the target line at impact.

Arms: Arms are opposite the right side of the torso at impact. Left arm has rotated and is virtually straight. It is to be flung across the chest. The right arm has started its release.

WARNING
Do not force your right elbow onto the front of your right hip. This move tends to put the clubhead behind you with the face open—in the "stuck" position that is the one-plane swinger's most common fault.

Hips: The hips should be open by 35 to 50 degrees in relation to the target line at impact, or slightly more open than the shoulders.

WARNING
Do not dramatically tilt the right hip down and the left hip up. Doing so will affect the other body parts and throw the club's movement off plane. Fat shots will commonly result.

Spine Angle: The spine should retain the same degree of forward bend as at address or even increase slightly. From a face-on view, the spine should show a very slight tilt to the player's right.

WARNING
Do not change the spine's forward bend.

Weight Distribution: Weight should be evenly distributed on both feet or slightly favoring the left leg.

WARNING
Do not slide laterally and shift too much weight left. The legs act as stabilizers for the turn of the upper body.

Club: The clubface is square. The club shaft is more upright than at address and leans slightly toward the target.

WARNING
Do not block with the hands and arms and attempt to hold the club on a straight line. (Keep the left arm rotating and the right arm releasing to allow the club to move on an arc.)

Two-Plane Impact

Shoulders: The shoulders should be either square to the target or slightly open.

WARNING
Do not exaggerate the turning action of the shoulders. (They should be passive.)

Arms: The arms are directly in front of the body or slightly to the right side of center, in a position similar to the address. The wrists should be fully uncocked.

WARNING
Do not let your arms get stuck behind your body.

Hips: Hips should be square to the target line or slightly open. The right hip is slightly lower than the left or lead hip.

WARNING
Do not turn the hips too vigorously lest they outpace the arms.

Spine Angle: From the down-target view, the spine should be angled forward the same amount as at address (10 to 20 degrees). From a face-on view, the spine should be tilted to the player's right the same amount (or slightly more) as at address.

WARNING
Do not let your spine angle change dramatically during the downswing.

Weight Distribution: Two-plane players should have 50–60 percent of their weight on the left or lead foot at impact. The left foot should be flat on the ground at impact.

WARNING
Do not shift your weight onto the outside of your left or lead foot. This indicates an overactive lateral lower-body shift and poor balance at impact.

Club: The clubface should be square to target. The club shaft should be at virtually the same angle as at address, rather than the butt end

THE ONE-PLANE ADDRESS:
Caught on Camera
The most critical points of the one-plane address for you to heed and form a visual picture of in your mind are: Peter Jacobsen's bent-over posture, fairly wide stance, slightly closed stance, and hands under the chin. More than anything else, this address will help promote a more rounded swing—sort of a baseball swing aimed at the ground.

THE ONE-PLANE BACKSWING:
Caught on Camera
In viewing these photographs of the one-plane backswing, pay close attention to how Peter swings his left arm across his chest, turns his shoulders on a fairly steep plane ninety degrees to his spine, and arrives at the top of the swing with his left wrist flat (rather than cupped) and the club shaft parallel to the target line.

THE ONE-PLANE DOWNSWING:
Caught on Camera
These photographs are all telling. The first really shows how the shoulders and upper torso unwind at the start of the downswing, with the arms and club being carried into the ideal hitting slot. The second photograph of Peter in the be-all-and-end-all impact zone shows how the torso and the rotating left arm carry the club down the plane line and fling it powerfully through the ball. Notice how early the clubhead has already moved left and back to the inside of his target line.

**THE TWO-PLANE
ADDRESS: Caught on
Camera**
The most critical points
of the two-plane setup
for you to heed and form
a visual picture of are:
Peter Jacobsen's erect
posture, fairly narrow
stance, and closeness
to the ball. More than
anything else, this
address helps promote
a more upright swing,
so vital to the two-plane
swing.

THE TWO-PLANE BACKSWING:
Caught on Camera
In viewing these photographs of the
two-plane swing, pay close attention
to how Peter's shoulders turn on a
flat plane and arms on a more
upright plane or angle. At the top of
the swing, note the across-the-line
position of the club, common to
two-plane golfers.

THE TWO-PLANE DOWNSWING:
Caught on Camera
These photographs are all telling.
The first shows how Peter's hips
begin to shift laterally immediately,
rather than rotate counterclockwise
or "clear," and the arms separate
downward from the right shoulder.
The second photograph of Peter in
the impact zone shows how the
spine angle tilts slightly more to the
right, the arms swing down in front
of the body, the wrists fully uncock
and, most importantly, the shoulders
rotate through pretty much the same
degree as the hips. As for the club,
notice how it has only moved slightly
left and back inside the target line,
indicating a straighter line swing
than the one-plane.

being higher as for the one-plane player. There may be a slight lean of the club shaft toward the target.

WARNING

Do not let the club shaft lean more than a few degrees toward the target. Also, it must never lean noticeably away from the target, or fat shots will result.

Into the Follow-Through

A graceful, well-balanced follow-through is very desirable, because it indicates that a well-balanced and well-timed swing preceded it. You'll rarely see a very good player with an ungainly follow-through, nor will you often see a poor golfer with a beautiful finish to the swing.

Some people may argue that the follow-through is not important because when you reach this point in the swing, the ball is long gone. That's true, but the follow-through is a mirror of what went before it. As such, it can be very instructive to look at. When we talk about the follow-through, let's make sure that one thing is clear: We are discussing the natural positions of the body and the golf club at the completion of the swing. We are not talking about an artificial pose that the golfer should try to assume at the end of his or her swing. I will often see amateurs who, halfway into a poorly balanced, out-of-position follow-through, will actually adjust themselves into what they think is a picture finish. It's as if they think that correcting their pose is going to help correct their shot. Of course it can't, but I guess you can't blame them for trying. This attempt at a correction shows that, at least on an instinctive level, they know they are ending up in an unbalanced position. But a belated fix of the follow-through does them no good. Swinging directly into a good follow-through would mean a lot more. Let's look at the correct follow-through positions of the one- and two-plane players. Though they both should look fluid, well balanced, and under control, you'll see that they are actually quite a bit different from one another.

It's important to note that when I describe the various body and club positions I will be describing them for the follow-through of a full swing with a driver. The player who is hitting a controlled shot with a lofted iron will not swing the body and the club as far around as described here. Likewise, the follow-through will vary somewhat depending on whether the player is trying to hit a specialty shot such as a low hook, a slice, a punch shot, or some other shot with an altered trajectory.

One more thing: There will be no review segment for the one-plane and two-plane swing follow-through positions simply because this part of the swing is a result of what came before. Still, it's important to learn the elements of a good follow-through so you'll be more apt to achieve one, again provided your swing is technically sound prior to that point.

The One-Plane Follow-Through

Shoulders

You may have heard or read that in the follow-through the front of your body should be facing the target. I feel that this is, at best, incomplete information. In fact, for the one-plane swinger in particular, this is erroneous instruction because it does not differentiate between the position of the shoulders and the position of the hips. At the finish, the one-plane player's shoulders should be fully and completely unwound to the left, or counterclockwise, for the right-handed player. You cannot turn your shoulders too far into the follow-through. However, the amount that they turn will obviously vary depending on your torso's strength and flexibility. Watch Michelle Wie or Ernie Els when they follow-through on a drive, particularly if it is on a long par-five where they know they must hit the ball extra hard to get home in two. Both of these great one-plane swingers will turn their shoulders far beyond the point where their shoulders face the target. Wie and Els can turn their shoulders nearly 90 degrees beyond where they face the target, or, to put it another way, they turn their shoulders nearly 180 degrees beyond where they were at the address position. But these are two of the most flexible and powerful players in golf. They turn their shoulders hard enough through the downswing that the shoulders just want to keep on going, and they are both flexible enough to let that happen.

You will also see many junior players who are flexible enough to attain a huge shoulder turn. Chances are, if you're an adult weekend amateur, your shoulders will not turn this far. The point is, though, that they should turn as far as they can. If your shoulders can reach the point where they are slightly beyond the point where they face the target—or, say, 100 degrees past their original square position at address—you've made a good turn to the finish.

When viewed either from up or down target line, a line across your shoulders should be horizontal or nearly horizontal to the ground. This is a result of the spine angle starting to straighten up just after impact and continuing to straighten as the shoulders unwind in the follow-through.

Arms

At the finish, the arms have been swung around by the force of your shoulder and torso turn and by the release of the right arm over the left arm. Instead of trailing the body, they now have been flung across the front of the chest and over to the left side. Your arm position is not quite a mirror image of your position at the top of the backswing. Because your spine is now erect as it nears the end of the follow-through, your right arm (for the right-handed player) is fully extended across your chest. Your right hand should be above your left shoulder and the left arm should be folded upward at the elbow.

Hips

The hips should be fully rotated toward the target. Again, precisely how much your hips turn depends on your flexibility. Ideally, they will face the target (which means your hips would be turned 90 degrees beyond their position at address) or even be turned slightly beyond or to the left of the target. When you compare the amount your hips are turned with your shoulder turn at the finish, your shoulders should be turned farther than your hips have turned.

Spine Angle

When viewed from up-target (that is, from the target looking back to the player), the player's spine angle should be fairly erect. It is acceptable for the spine to be tilted slightly to the player's right, or toward the target line. This slight tilt is acceptable for the one-plane player because this player's shoulders turn on a steeper plane than the two-plane swinger's, whose shoulder plane is nearly horizontal.

I'd like to add one important point about the spine angle at the finish, and this applies equally to the two-plane player. When viewed from face-on to the address position, the player's spine at follow-through should appear erect. It should not be tilted backward, that is, the top of the spine should not be farther from the target than the base of the spine. Such a backward tilting of the spine indicates that an exaggerated sliding move by the hips and the legs occurred during the swing. Such a move would be especially destructive to the action of a one-plane swing. Perhaps more importantly, this backward spine tilt is the basis for what is known as the "reverse C" finish position, which I have discussed previously. Over time, swinging into the reverse C will put enormous strain on your lower back. It may not start hurting until you're older, but believe me, at some point you will develop back problems. Tom Kite and Peter Jacobsen are perhaps the best example of players who developed from two-plane swingers into wonderful one-plane swingers and who, in the process, went from having a big reverse C to having a very erect spine at the finish.

Weight Distribution

At the finish, the one-plane player's weight should be almost entirely on the left or forward foot. The left leg should be straight while the right leg is slightly bent. The right knee should be slightly bent, with the right lower leg angled forward and the player up on the right toe.

Club

At the finish, the hands and the club will come around in a slightly lower position for the one-plane swinger than the two-planer. This is consistent with the somewhat flatter overall swing plane of the one-plane player. This player's hands should be just above and slightly outside the point of the left shoulder. The club should be behind the player's upper back, with the clubhead only slightly lower than the butt end of the club, which is the same as saying that the club shaft is nearly horizontal to the ground.

A note here, particularly for you serious golfers who like to use video or photography. Just after impact, in the early part of the follow-through, the clubhead, when viewed from down the target line, should first appear in photographs to come left of the body just under or below the left shoulder. This is a very important point because it shows the arms and club have been slung around the torso to the left, and not out and up away from it. If the arms and club are not slung around like a baseball bat, with the right arm releasing over the left arm, they will drift out and away from the torso. The club will break the arc and stay on too straight a line, going too far down the target line. This fault will result in pushes and hooks or, if the hands are blocking to hold off the hook, heel or shank shots.

A great deal of misinformation exists regarding swinging the club down the target line as long as possible. This couldn't be farther from the truth. Remember, you are playing a side-on game, and all golf swings, regardless of one- or two-plane, must move in an arc from inside the target line to the target line and then back to the inside again. The two-plane swing will do this less than the one-plane swing because of its more upright nature. However, I would strongly advise you to ignore any golf instruction that suggests swinging on a straight line toward your target. That's good information for an on-line game such as darts or croquet, but it is disastrous for any side-on game such as baseball, tennis, or golf.

The Two-Plane Follow-Through

Shoulders

The shoulders of the two-plane golfer turn through the downswing along with the hips, rather than winding against the hips both at the top of the backswing and in the follow-through. However, it is less likely that the two-plane swinger will generate as much shoulder turn in the follow-through as I described for the supple one-plane swinger. This is because the shoulders, which are not the main power source in the two-plane swing, are held back somewhat on the downswing and therefore do not have as much momentum through impact and into the follow-through. So the two-plane player who has good flexibility should finish with his or her shoulders facing the target. It is less likely that the two-planer's shoulder turn can go beyond this point. But the majority of players should be able to end up with their shoulders facing or nearly facing the target at the finish.

When viewed from an up-target vantage point, your shoulders should appear level or horizontal. This is even truer for the two-plane golfer, because your spine angle has been far less bent over during the swing and will probably be even more erect at the finish than the one-plane swinger's.

Arms

The position of the arms in the two-plane follow-through is noticeably different from the one-plane follow-through. The right arm should be just slightly bent. The left arm, meanwhile, is bent so that the upper arm is at about a 90-degree angle to the forearm. Both arms are in a substantially more upright finish position in the two-plane swing. The right arm is swung more upward than horizontally. The hands are directly above the left shoulder or even above the inside of the neck. Colin Montgomerie and Hale Irwin are great examples of this high finish with the hands and arms.

Hips

The two-plane player's hips should be turned virtually the same amount as the shoulders in the follow-through, so that they are more or less facing the target.

Spine Angle

There may be a slight difference in the two-plane golfer's spine angle at the finish. This player's spine should be perfectly vertical, as opposed to the slight lean to the player's right that I mentioned for the one-plane golfer. It's extremely important that the two-plane golfer's spine remain upright, because any leaning toward the player's right indicates that he or she was tilting rather than turning through the downswing.

When viewed from face-on to the address position, again, the spine at follow-through should be perfectly vertical rather than tilted backward. Again, this puts you in excellent balance and greatly reduces the strain on your lower back.

Weight Distribution

There is no difference at the finish between the weight distributions of the one- and two-plane swingers. Good balance is good balance no matter what method you choose to swing the club with. Again, your weight should be nearly 100 percent on your left or front leg. That left leg should be straight, while your right side is up on the toe of your golf shoe, with the right leg bent forward fairly noticeably.

Club

The manner in which the club hangs in the follow-through is another obvious point of difference. The two-planer, whose hands are higher, should have the club dropping behind his or her back at an angle that is closer to vertical than the one-plane player will—say, 60 to 70 degrees down from horizontal. From an up-target vantage point, the part of the club shaft that you can see below the hands will be dropping down behind the middle of the player's shoulder or even behind the inside part of the neck.

Here's something you serious golfers who use video or photography should note. The clubhead when viewed in photographs from down the target line will first appear in the early stages of the follow-through to be at the left shoulder or just above it, between the shoulder and the neck. This is considerably higher and less around than the one-plane swing. The two-plane is more upright, and as a result the clubhead should first appear in a position that is higher and less around.

I also want to make a note here on the clubface as it first appears in these down-the-target-line photos for both the one- and two-plane swings. The clubface on both swings when executed correctly and on plane will be square to the plane (slightly left of "toe up") at that point. If it is not square at that point, it will either be too closed (face pointed to the ground) or too open (toe pointed to the sky). These two non-square clubfaces are very indicative of the swing being in the wrong direction coming into impact. The closed clubface shows a swing that is approaching impact from too far inside and is usually too far under as well, with the clubface too open. The golfer must use excessive hand manipulation to roll the club over to get it into the back of the ball. This excessive and last-minute rollover continues into the follow-through and is illustrated by the closed clubface. Conversely, the open clubface in the follow-through is usually the result of an out-to-in, over-the-top swing mistake, where the golfer must open the clubface in an effort to hit the back of the ball.

5

Practice Drills

Swing exercises you can do at home or on the driving range, designed to help you groove the proper on-plane movements and correct common faults

I suspect that when you, the golfer-reader, turn the page of an instruction book and see a heading with the word *drills* in it, you automatically think to yourself, "Maybe I'll just skip this section."

I can understand any unwillingness that you might have, because if you have played the game for any length of time, you have probably heard of and tried a great many drills. And I will certainly admit that there have been quite a number of drills that various teachers have professed to be cure-alls for an "ill" golf swing. The irony is that, in many cases, these drills have actually done more harm than good to the swings of many golfers. But if you will bear with me for a few moments, no matter which type of swing you decide to employ, I will convince you that drills can be both fun and useful in learning a new swing or fixing a faulty one.

The first thing I'd like you to do is realize that, if you want to improve your golf swing, you have to work at it. I don't necessarily mean that you have to go to the practice range and hit 500 balls every day. Even if you wanted to do that, it's highly unlikely that you could. Chances are that you are an amateur golfer who plays the game as often as your schedule permits, given the responsibilities of your occupation, family, and other meaningful activities. Some of you may be able to play three rounds a week and hit balls a couple of times a week. Other readers may only play 15 to 20 rounds a year, much as you might like to play more. But regardless of your individual circumstances, if you want to improve your game, you need to take specific steps to permanently ingrain into your swing the various movements and positions that I have previously described.

Still, at this point you might be asking, "Do I *have* to do these drills, and, if so, how often?" My answer is this: You should only do these drills if you want to hit better, more solid, more accurate golf shots, which will translate into substantially lower golf scores. I think that this is probably what you are hoping to accomplish; otherwise, you would not have read up to this point. Spending time on these drills will help.

Once you understand which fundamentals belong in your swing, you should see immediate improvement. The proof will be the improvement in the flight of the ball. One thing that I firmly believe is that whenever a student takes a formal lesson, at the end of that lesson, the player should be striking the ball better than when he or she arrived. I am not one of those teachers who tells players that their shots are going to get worse before they eventually get better. If the quality of your shots is not better after you try to implement what the teacher has communicated to you, then at least one of three things is not right:

1. You do not fully understand what the teacher is trying to communicate.
2. You are not doing exactly what the instructor has told you to do.
3. What the instructor has told you to do was not correct to begin with.

Practicing the drills or practice exercises contained in this chapter will certainly help you to understand what I'm trying to communicate. They are all clear and simple to execute, so you will have no trouble following my directions. I am certain that after working steadfastly on these drills and then starting to hit actual shots as you ingrain each vital move into your new one- or two-plane golf swing, your progress will be accelerated.

It will encourage you greatly to know that a vast majority of the players on the PGA Tour have several favorite practice drills that they use whenever the opportunity arises. I mentioned, previously, how one-plane swingers Scott McCarron and Peter Jacobsen, among others, take a towel or a head cover and hold it between their left upper arm and chest as they make a practice swing. Let me assure you, the best players in the world are willing to use any drill that helps them feel the correct movements in the swing or fix a fault in their one- or two-plane technique. There isn't a player on the PGA Tour who thinks he is too good to work on swing improvement drills, including Tiger Woods, Vijay Singh, and Phil Mickelson. After you study the following drills and think about them a bit, I think you will agree that they are simple and sensible in what they will help you accomplish and are certainly worth a try.

Four of the following eight drills are directed at the one-plane swinger, and four are meant for the two-planer. Do not practice all eight of the drills. If you are trying to produce a one-plane swing, do only the four designed to ingrain the specific movements of your personal action. If you opt for the two-plane swing, work only on the four drills designed to improve that swing type.

Within each set of four drills, you will see that there are two drills that help you learn the correct body-turn movements for the one-plane and two-plane swings. Then there are two drills that help develop the correct arm swing for each method. The purpose of each drill is described, along with the procedure itself and a note on the type of ball-flight flaw or flaws that the drill will help you correct.

One-Plane Swing Drills

On-Plane Shoulder Turn Drill

Purpose: To develop a turn of the shoulders that stays on plane throughout the swing. This drill specifically checks whether the shoulders are on plane at the top of the backswing and at the point of impact.

Procedure: You will need an assistant to help you with this drill, which is best performed with a long iron. While standing erect, hold the club with your left hand so that the clubhead is against the top of your sternum. The grip end of the club should extend horizontally outward, across and beyond your right shoulder. Because a long iron is between 38 and 40 inches long, the butt of the club should extend some 28 to 30 inches beyond the shirt seam on your right shoulder.

Next, bend your spine forward so that your body (except for your arms) is in a normal address posture for, say, a medium or long iron. Your goal is to make a backswing and downswing shoulder turn that is within the parameters of the desired plane for the one-plane swinger. This is where your assistant comes in. He or she should stand in front of you and hold either a middle or long iron at arm's length, with the grip end pointing vertically downward. The grip end should be directly over the spot at which the ball would be located. The middle of the grip should be approximately knee height. To execute this drill correctly, it is critical that this vertical club be positioned precisely as described. That's because this club will act as an indicator of whether your shoulders are turning on plane. If this indicator is not positioned correctly, then the feedback you get from this drill will also be inaccurate.

Okay, you are in your address posture, holding your own club horizontally across your right or rear shoulder. From here, simply turn your shoulders as you would in making a normal backswing, while keeping your club in position against the right shoulder. From this top-of-the-backswing position, an imaginary line extension of the club you are holding should point through the left shoulder and into the imaginary four-foot zone outside the ball, as discussed earlier. From here, turn your shoulders freely and fully down and through an imaginary impact and follow-through. As you do this, the grip end of your club should strike the grip end of the club your partner is dangling above the ball's position. It will only do so if your shoulders have turned along the acceptable plane line for the one-plane player, which we discussed earlier—that is, a plane that runs down from the shoulders into the zone just outside the ball. You see, the club that you're holding beyond your right shoulder serves as an extension or a visible indicator of the plane line your shoulders are turning on. At the simulated point of impact, if your grip contacts the grip end of the club dangling above the imaginary ball, you can see that if the line formed by the club were extended to the ground, it would touch the ground at a point in the zone that is outside the ball's

Photos 5.1–5.3 On-Plane Shoulder Turn Drill: Step One (left); Step Two (center); Step Three (right).

position, but not more than the 48-inch zone outside the ball. Thus, you know that, at impact, your shoulders have turned on plane.

Conversely, if your club's grip does not hit the grip your partner is holding, you know you are not swinging on the desired plane. If your club hits your partner's club on the club shaft, above the grip, it indicates that you've turned your shoulders on too flat of a plane, too horizontally for a one-plane swing. If the opposite occurs—that is, your club passes below the grip on your partner's club—it means your shoulders are tilting or turning too steeply or in too much of an upright manner.

There's a good tip to be learned here, especially if you feel as if you turned your shoulders at right angles to your spine, yet your club still didn't strike the vertical club in its grip area: It's possible that you did make a turn that was at a right angle to your spine. However, your spine angle at address was incorrect. You may simply need to tilt your spine more forward or less forward at address, and then make exactly the same movement to create a shoulder turn that is perfectly on plane.

If your spine angle at address was correct and your club's grip is still not contacting the grip end of the dangling club, this tells you that you are tilting your shoulders in some fashion during the swing, rather than turning them. If you dip your right shoulder at the start of the downswing, which many golfers do, your shoulder turn coming into the ball will be too steep and your club will pass underneath the vertical club. If you move your head forward on the downswing and lunge at the ball, which is another very common fault, your right shoulder will move farther outward and higher than it should be, so your club will hit the vertical club somewhere up on the shaft. So this drill will also indicate if you're not holding your head steady throughout the swing motion. Keeping the head steady, I should note, is something that is required to successfully complete every one-plane drill I will show you.

The On-Plane Shoulder Turn Drill immediately shows you if something is amiss either in your setup posture or in the shoulder turn itself. If you have trouble making grip-to-grip contact, ask your partner for feedback as to which of the flaws I've described is the likely culprit. Then, make the adjusted shoulder-turn motion. Once you have your shoulders turning on plane, repeat the drill at least 10 times. This entire process should take you no more than two minutes or so, even if you are not turning on plane at the start. Once you have this drill down pat, I recommend that you repeat it periodically, preferably in front of a mirror, at least once per week, to make sure you are continuing to make a correct, on-plane shoulder turn and have not fallen back into any previous bad habits.

Ball-Flight Correction: Learning how to turn your shoulders in a one-plane swing is especially helpful to golfers who come over the top. These golfers tend to hit either pulled shots or pull-slices. An over-the-top, outside-in path also can cause skied shots because this swing path is inherently steeper than it should be. With an on-plane shoulder turn, your clubhead will move on a path from inside to along the target line at impact, then return to the inside after impact. The result will be a shot that starts on your target line or a shade right of the target with a straight flight or a slight right-to-left draw.

Oblique Abs Turn-Strengthener Drill

Purpose: This is an excellent combination drill-exercise designed to strengthen your body turn both away from the ball and down and through the impact zone, thus adding speed and power to your swing.

Procedure: The muscles you will be focusing on are the oblique abdominal muscles, which are the patches of muscle located on either side of your abdomen. These are the muscles that rotate the middle and upper torso.

There are exactly two ways to do this drill and any number of options on how much weight, if any, you want to use. So, any way that you do this exercise, you will be able to measure just how much you have improved your oblique abdominal strength.

The first way to do this exercise is on a gym machine specifically designed to work the oblique abdominal muscles. If you happen to be a member of a local gym, you are probably quite familiar with it. With the standard oblique abdominal machine, you will begin in a sitting position. The machine will have two pads attached to levers on either side of you at about ear height. You place your hands on the outsides of these pads and then push them together, so that your hands are in front of you, palms facing.

From here, your task is to simply turn your body to your right, from the waist up, as a right-handed player would turn for the backswing. Make sure to turn as far as you can. You will feel tension in your oblique abdominal muscles from resistance coming from the weight of the apparatus. From there, turn back through your original starting position, turning as far as you can to your left. This motion mimics the downswing and follow-through. Make sure to make each turn fully and slowly. As you turn left, you'll again build up tension in the oblique abs.

I should mention that, before you begin working out, you should set the machine to add any amount of weight that you want to the resistance to your turn. The weights are usually connected to the apparatus by means of a pulley system. On most machines you can start with no added weight if you wish or add as much as you can handle in 10-pound increments. It's a great exercise machine.

A good question you might have is, "How much weight should I use?" If you have never used an oblique abdominal machine before, I recommend that you begin with no weight added on, get yourself settled into the machine correctly, take the position described, and then do one complete turn in each direction. If it's obvious that this is not a sufficient amount of resistance, start adding some weight, but do so very gradually. Everybody is different. Some people find that adding 10 to 20 pounds is plenty at the start, and there may be others who can do this exercise using 70, 80, even 100 pounds of resistance. My advice is to find a weight level at which you can do 12 full repetitions (turning in both directions) comfortably. Then do three to five sets of 12 reps. If and when this starts to feel rather easy, increase the weight by 10 pounds. But it's much easier to do more repetitions with less weight than to strain with too much weight and risk injury.

There is a simple way to do this exercise at home, without the benefit of an ab machine in the gym. Here's how.

Put your hands against your abs and lower ribs, with your fingers pointing downward and your elbows pointing out. Bend forward from the waist by about 30 degrees, much as you would at address. Next, simply make the same moves that you would when using the abdominal machine, turning first to the right, then back as far as you can to the left. Again, do 12 full, slow repetitions.

If you find that doing the exercise in this manner is not taxing enough, you can up the ante, so to speak, by holding a flat plate weight against your chest or by holding hand weights in each hand while still resting your hands on the sides of your torso. This will toughen the exercise considerably, so you probably will not need much weight. Peter Jacobsen does this drill while holding a 10-pound dumbbell in each hand. That is a lot of weight to carry, not only for the strain it puts on your abs but also on your hands and forearms. I would recommend that if you need some weight, start with a five-pound plate weight or a two- to five-pound dumbbell in each hand. Make the same full, slow turns in both directions, and do three sets of 12 repetitions. If you find you can increase the weight over time, that's fine. But don't push it. You might move up to a seven- or eight-pound weight in each hand and perhaps eventually 10 pounds. Just keep doing plenty of repetitions and you'll add plenty of speed to your turn through the ball.

Ball-Flight Correction: This drill does not alter any curvature of the ball per se. What it does is add explosiveness to your swing and, with it, increased clubhead speed for a longer carry with any club in the bag.

Elbows Up, Arms Across Drill

Purpose: The purpose of this drill is to teach you precisely how the arms should move during the one-plane swing. The movements of the arms are the opposite of each other in what each does during the backswing and the downswing.

Procedure: There are several parts or options to this drill. The first part is to train both arms in a slightly exaggerated manner as to how they will bend during the swing. With a bent-over spine angle and your arms hanging down in front of you, lift your upper arms while simultaneously bending the elbows. Your upper arms should be angled back with both

Photo 5.4 **From this position, simply turn back then through, feeling how the elbows work during the Elbow Up, Arms Across Drill, and, of course, during the swing.**

elbows pointing straight behind you. In addition to your upper arms moving up and behind you, make sure that the elbows have moved to or just past the seams at the sides of your shirt. Also make sure that there is an inch or two between the inside of each biceps and the sides of your chest. This is important because in the actual swing, you will need the arms slightly away from the body to facilitate your freedom of movement.

This up-and-back thrust you have made is precisely how your arms should work on either side of the ball. On the backswing, your right arm will be making this up-and-back movement. Then, starting just before impact and continuing into the follow-through, it will be the left arm that goes up and back. Move your arms behind you in this fashion 10 times, making the motion fairly slowly, holding the position for one second and then lowering your arms back in front of you.

The second part of this drill is to practice what the opposite arm is doing when one arm is folding. As your right arm folds on the backswing, your left moves horizontally across your chest and rotates so the left forearm is somewhat facing the sky. From a standing position, simply swing your left arm up and rotate it across your chest. As you make this move, your left biceps muscle should press firmly against your left pectoral (chest) muscle. Move your left arm up in this fashion, hold for one second, and then return it to your side. Repeat this exercise 10 times. Then reverse this drill, extending and rotating your right arm horizontally across your chest, with the right biceps pressing against your right pectoral muscle. This is how your right arm should move just beyond the impact zone and into the follow-through, while your left arm is folding up and back. Again, repeat this right-arm-across-the-chest action 10 times.

In addition to practicing these singular arm positions as described, you should also practice the Elbows Up, Arms Across Drill while holding a club. Just fold your right arm up and back as described on the backswing, with your left arm rotating and pressing horizontally against your chest. Then reverse the move for the downswing, with your right arm rotating and crossing the chest while the left arm folds up and back.

Finally, once you have started feeling comfortable with these slightly exaggerated arm movements, you can practice this drill while hitting some chip and pitch shots. As you get the feel of the movement in miniature, so to speak, you can gradually incorporate these movements into some very compact punch-type shots. Use a seven- or eight-iron. As you hit these shots, focus solely on the correct arm movements. Make sure to keep your hands and wrists very firm throughout this short swing.

Ball-Flight Correction: By teaching one arm to bend upward and backward while the opposite arm is swinging across the chest, this drill is very helpful to the golfer who keeps both arms too much in front of the body throughout the swing. Again, keeping the arms in front of the

Photos 5.5 and 5.6 **To get a good feel for how the left arm and right arm work during the Elbows Up, Arms Across Drill and during a short compact swing, practice swinging back (left) then through (right) with a club in your hand. Concentrate on how the elbows hinge and the arms move across your chest—first the right elbow and left arm on the backswing, then the left elbow and right arm on the downswing.**

chest is desirable only if you are striving to develop a two-plane rather than a one-plane swing. A player bent over in a one-plane posture, keeping his or her arms on front of their chest, will have a narrow swing arc — that is, the club will move up from and back down to the ball on a steep angle. When the arc is too narrow, flush contact is very hard to obtain, and both fat and thin shots tend to be the result. The Elbows Back, Arms Across Drill teaches the golfer to develop the correct one-plane arm action. This, in turn, makes it easier for the golfer to drive the clubhead squarely into the back of the ball, providing maximum distance as well as more consistent distances with every club.

One-Plane Release Drill

Purpose: The purpose of this drill is to train your hands and arms to work correctly through the impact zone in the one-plane swing. The arms are somewhat active during the impact zone while the hands are essentially passive in the one-plane swing. However, the hands and arms must describe a specific arc through the impact zone. If the arc of the hands and arms is consistent, then the clubhead will also follow a consistent arc or path to meet the ball squarely.

Procedure: Before we get started with the movements in this drill, you need to understand a few terms regarding the movement of your hands, arms, and the club through the impact zone. We are going to discuss the path of the hands and arms along what I call the "inner circle" and the clubhead along what I call the "outer circle."

Imagine that, when you're over the ball, there's a curved line on the ground in front of your feet. This line begins a bit behind your right foot then curves outward in front of your feet by several inches. Then the line curves back around to the outside of your left foot. This is the *inner circle* of the impact zone. Your hands should move directly over this imaginary portion of a circle.

Without using a club, bend your spine and place your hands and arms opposite your right side. Your right elbow should be positioned behind your right hip, against your right side, not in front of your right hip. Practice moving your hands smoothly above this inner circle. Actually, your hips, shoulders, and arms will supply some of the energy to move your hands along the path of the inner circle. Make sure that in all parts of this drill you keep your hands and wrists very firm. Keep moving your hips, shoulders, arms, and hands back and forth over this imaginary line. Notice that, at the start, with your hands opposite your right side, you can get your hands back around almost to impact by just turning your hips and shoulders. Notice also how, at the point just before impact, your arms start to move across your torso from the right side to the left while you still turn your body and your hands still stay over the inner circle. While your arms are moving around and across your torso, your hips and shoulders continue to turn.

The particular part of the arms moving across your torso that deserves attention is the left biceps, the left forearm, and the right arm. At the top of the backswing and during the downswing, the left biceps is approximately opposite the middle of your chest. Just before impact it begins to move left, across your chest toward the left side of your torso. Its ultimate position is discussed in the Elbows Up, Arms Across Drill. While this is occurring, the left forearm continues to rotate and the right arm straightens.

Does this movement of your hands feel exactly like it does when you are making your normal swing? Chances are it won't. Most golfers tend to use too much independent wrist action in the impact zone. The body and arm motion, beyond what is mentioned above, will be the amount needed when you have a club in your hands to bring the clubface "square" and out onto the outer circle. Your hands are now moving along a circular path. There will be some movement down and then back up again, as you move down and then up the plane from the right to the left on the circle. The majority of golfers will move their hands down and through impact on a straighter line than the inner circle I've described. If your hands move through impact on a straighter line, it means that the clubhead will be forced to move into impact either off plane or in the wrong direction.

Next, take a middle iron in hand and set up in the one-plane address position. Move your hands back to be opposite your right side with your right elbow behind your hip, not in front. Then turn through, letting your arms release across your torso, all the while keeping your hands

Photos 5.7 and 5.8 **To educate your hands and train them to work correctly in the one-plane swing, practice moving them over what I refer to as the swing's "inner circle."**

above the inner circle. Repeat this movement at least a dozen times. As you get the feel of this, note how the clubhead is moving. You'll see that it's moving on an arc that is of the same shape as the inner circle but is well outside your hands. The arc on the ground underneath where your clubhead is moving is what I call the *outer circle*. As you move your hands the relatively short distance described over the inner circle, the clubhead will automatically travel along the much larger arc of the outer circle. In actual play, all you have to do is bend over sufficiently and stand the correct distance from the ball for the shot at hand (which is another way of saying the ball would be located at or near the top of the outer circle). Then simply turn your hips and your shoulders on plane and release your arms and hands along the inner circle, and your clubhead will move much more quickly through impact with the ball. Once again, there must be enough rotation of the left forearm that the shaft moves out in front of the arms and the clubface, as it reaches the start of the outer circle, is square to that portion of the circle. Any left-arm rotation from that point on is just to ensure that your clubhead stays on the outer circle and that you maintain a square clubface to the arc, not to the target. The clubface that is square to the arc will be moving from open to closed in relation to the target. If there is insufficient left-arm rotation in an actual swing, the club will be held too far behind the arms, with the clubface too open. As the arms approach impact, the right arm begins to straighten and swing on the arc to the left.

Practice this movement of your arms and the club as often as you can. Keep an eye peeled on the clubhead as you do this to make sure it is staying on that outer circle. Keep working your arms and the club until the movement begins to feel natural.

The movement of your arms and the clubhead I've described is really a simple matter of physics. Your arms are acting as the inner or centripetal force. They are closer to the hub of the swing (your torso) and as such are moving with as much speed as you can muster. However, the speed of your arms is just a small fraction of the speed imparted to the clubhead. The clubhead receives the outer or centrifugal effect from the centripetal force. As your arms swing and release around and inward across your torso, the clubhead is thrown outward and into the ball at

Photos 5.9–5.11 The more advanced stage of the One-Plane Release Drill involves simultaneously swinging the hands along the inner circle and the club along the outer circle.

tremendous speed. The action is much like that of a Ferris wheel or a merry-go-round, where the energy imparted from the inner force is distributed and greatly multiplied in the outward effect (the clubhead).

Again, move your hips, shoulders, and arms as quickly as you can. Note that as you make this move, your right hand should not completely cross over your left. Keep the hands firm. In the one-plane swing, the crossover does occur, but it should not take place until farther into the follow-through, when your hands are above waist height. (As we'll see shortly, the two-plane swing has a much more active release.)

Finally, once you have the feel of the one-plane release with a club in your hands, go ahead and hit some short shots using this move. You'll start to see that the contact between the clubface and the ball will become more consistent the more you do this drill.

Ball-Flight Correction: While the One-Plane Release Drill will help you consistently make square contact with the ball, it is particularly helpful to amateurs who have trouble controlling the direction of the clubface at impact (an open clubface at impact causing a push or slice; a closed clubface at impact contributing to a pull or hook). By setting up squarely to your target and then ingraining the one-plane release, you can expect to hit all your full shots with a ball flight that is very close to straight. It is also a very good way to learn the low, driven punch shot that is particularly useful in the wind.

Two-Plane Swing Drills

Before I begin discussing drills to help all of you two-plane swingers develop the desired motion, let me reiterate that the one-plane golfer should work with only the drills on the previous pages. If you are a two-plane swinger (or plan to be), then focus only on the four upcoming drills.

Full-Body Turn Drill

Purpose: To train the golfer how to create a full-body turn on the backswing and the downswing, using the shoulders, torso, and hips to the fullest extent.

Procedure: Take a club and assume your normal setup position, without a ball. Remember that, as a two-plane swinger, you will be standing fairly erect, with just a slight forward bend from the waist. This drill will break down the movements of the body into three parts. You should mentally count "one-two-three" as you execute each move.

Count One: Simulate a backswing by turning your upper body to the right (for a right-handed golfer) as fully as possible. You want to get your entire upper body, from head through midsection, behind an imaginary line drawn vertically up from the golf ball as you reach the top-of-the-backswing position.

As you turn, your hips will turn a good deal more than the one-plane golfer's. Do not try to limit the turn of the hips, but merely let them follow the upper body.

An important point to highlight here is that it is acceptable if your head (and with it your shoulders) moves a little bit to your right (for a right-handed player). Remember, the two-plane swing inherently tends to be narrow. Moving your head to the right just a little will add some width to your swing arc. I'm not recommending a conscious sway to the right, but if your head does move a little bit laterally away from the target as you make a big turn, that's acceptable. Keep in mind that the hips and the legs, however, should not slide laterally.

Count Two: From your position at the top, your second step is to make a slight lateral slide of your left hip toward the target. This second step is a conscious move that comes after you have completed your backswing turn. Remember, in the two-plane swing, your backswing can come to a definite stop at the top before your initiate the downswing. That's because you have not wound your upper body against your hips, and thus you won't have that tension in your lower back like the one-plane player. So slide that hip just a few inches directly toward the target as you count "two." Note that, as you do this, you will feel some weight shift onto your left or forward foot, which will move back to flat on the ground. Also, as you make this move, make certain that you keep your shoulders quiet. It's very easy to tilt your

Photo 5.12 When practicing the Full-Body Turn Drill, count "one" as you turn your body fully away from an imaginary target.

Photo 5.13 When practicing the Full-Body Turn Drill, count "two" as you slide your left hip laterally toward the target.

Photo 5.14 When practicing the Full-Body Turn Drill, count "three" as you turn your hips and shoulders into the follow-through position.

shoulders as you employ this downswing trigger, with your right shoulder dipping downward. Do not allow this tilt to occur. It's helpful to do this drill in front of a mirror so you can check that your rear shoulder does not tilt down. A useful variation of count "two" is to allow your left foot to step toward the target along with the left hip.

Count Three: Right after you slide your left hip, count "three" as you simply turn your hips and shoulders together through the downswing and into the follow-through. The movement should feel full, free flowing, and easy, with no sense of holding anything back. Just turn fully through the ball so you finish with your belt buckle facing the target and your shoulders turned so they're also facing the target.

Now that you know all three parts of the drill, I recommend that at first you practice each move slowly, pausing between count one and count two and between count two and count three. Practice this drill in segments as long as you need to, until your body has memorized each move. In most cases, this will not be a lengthy process. You may feel you know how to move into each position with as few as 10 to 15 repetitions. When you gain a good feel for each proper action, start blending the three parts into one continuous, uninterrupted, rhythmic motion, counting "one-two-three" to yourself as you move through each position. Finally, I recommend that you always do the Full-Body Turn Drill more slowly than the speed of your real swing. Remember, rhythm and timing are more important ingredients in the two-plane swing. Staying smooth and feeling as though you're in slower-than-normal motion will help you when you bring your swing to the course.

Ball-Flight Correction: This is an excellent drill for any two-plane golfer who tends to come over the top on the downswing, with the resulting shot usually being either a pull, a slice, or, because this path is also a steep path, a skied shot. Making the first move down with a slight lateral slide of the left hip and then turning the entire body through the shot will ensure that the clubhead moves into the impact zone from slightly inside the target line. The result will be a straight shot or, if anything, one that draws a touch from right to left. Also, the swing path will be shallower, providing a more level hit for maximum power.

Anti-Tilt Drill

Purpose: This practice exercise, which I sometimes also refer to as the Helicopter Drill, is designed to keep the golfer's shoulders turning on the correct plane rather than tilting during the swing. This drill is especially effective for the two-plane golfer.

Procedure: Stand upright and hold both arms straight out to either side of you. Slowly turn your upper body to the right while keeping your arms out and straight. Then, after a slight pause, turn your upper body fully around to the left. Throughout this turning motion and at the completion of it, both arms should still be straight out and at shoulder level. If they are, it means you've turned your shoulders 90 degrees to your spine on a desirable, level plane. It will help as you work on this drill to think of your arms as wings and that you want to keep those wings level at all times.

If at any point in your turn you tilt either shoulder, it should be obvious because one of your hands will dip while the other reaches higher. For a right-handed player, the most obvious tendency will be to dip the right shoulder early in the downswing (so the right hand goes down while the left rises). This seems to be an instinctive move in which the golfer feels the need to move the club toward the ball by lowering the right shoulder. This move destroys the plane of the swing, because it moves the club too much behind and too much from the inside.

However, I should add that there are also a fair number of golfers who tilt the left or forward shoulder downward during the backswing. When they do so at the top of the backswing, their weight is on the left or forward foot. The Anti-Tilt Drill makes this fault obvious as well. Whatever the flaw you tend to have in your shoulder turn, this drill will help you quickly overcome it.

Two-planers should spend a few minutes with this drill just moving the shoulders and arms in both directions. Once the correct movement feels like second nature, you can combine this drill with the Full-Body Turn Drill. Instead of holding a club, just extend your arms as described and execute that drill's three steps. You are now ingraining the body's movement in the two-plane swing, while also making the desired shoulder turn.

Ball-Flight Correction: Golfers who tilt their shoulders on the backswing will struggle with a reverse pivot and an overly narrow swing arc.

Photos 5.15–5.17 If you are like the majority of amateur golfers who reverse pivot on the backswing, concentrate on this segment of the Anti-Tilt or Helicopter Drill: Start with your arms extended outward at your sides (left), then turn away keeping your arms out and straight (right). If you look like I do (below), you are still reverse pivoting and need to start over.

If this is your problem, you will tend to bring the club through impact on too steep an angle and, as a result, hit a steep top shot or sky ball or take too deep a divot. If you tilt during the downswing, you will usually get stuck too far from the inside with a shallow angle. You are likely to hit fat or thin shots because the bottom of the swing will occur behind the ball. Even if the shot is neither fat nor thin, it will lack power and have a very weak trajectory because the contact between the clubface and the ball was not clean. You can also hit pushes and hooks because a downswing tilt, once again, usually results in a swing path that is too much from in to out. This drill will help greatly in training you to make square and solid contact at impact and produce a driving ball flight that provides maximum carry and overall distance.

Arm Swing V Drill

Purpose: To train the two-plane swinger to make the correct motion of the arms during the backswing, through impact, and up into the follow-through. Unlike their movement in the one-plane action, both arms must be trained to stay in front of the body during the entire swing.

Procedure: As you'll recall, for the one-plane swing, the basic movement of the arms on either side of the ball is to lift your upper arms so that the elbows are pulled up and behind you. In the two-plane swing, there is a basic difference in the movement of the arms. You should lift your hands on either side of your shoulders, with your elbows bent and pointed somewhat down. In other words, with the two-plane swing, your elbows are pointed somewhat down rather than pointed back behind you as in the one-plane swing.

The motion of both arms during the swing is a steep, chopping movement. Assume your address position with an iron club. (A variation of this drill would have you take your address position without a club and to back up against a wall so that your buttocks are about a foot from the wall.) For a right-handed player, the first move is to lift your right arm up into the backswing position, elbow bent and pointing somewhat downward. Because your left hand is also on the club, it will simply go along for the ride. As you complete the upward arm move, both of your

Photos 5.18 and 5.19 The Arm Swing V Drill trains you to feel the correct positions and sensations as the club moves up (left) and through (right). The drill requires you to employ an up-and-down movement as if you are drawing an imaginary V in front of your torso.

hands will be in front of your right shoulder, with the club shaft pointing up over your right shoulder. To someone observing you from the face-on vantage point, it should appear as if your hands have moved along a line that would form the left-hand side of the letter V.

I'd like to interject a point here. If you execute this move as described, you may note that your left arm might be slightly bent rather than straight. This of course means that, in your real swing, the left arm might also be slightly bent, sort of like Curtis Strange's in his prime. This is permissible according to the two-plane principles I propose to students. I mention this technical point because many golfers have been advised to keep their left arm straight at the top of the backswing. I prefer a somewhat straight but not locked arm. However, some golfers cannot make the V move and cannot keep their arms in front of their torso without bending their left arm slightly.

The second arm movement is a steep downward chopping motion. In your actual swing, this motion must be performed in coordination with the turn of your body back down and through. Your right arm again provides part of the impetus by uncocking your right elbow.

Your left arm is also working in a downward swinging motion along with the unleashing of the right. Thus, both hands drive straight back down that left side of the letter V, which puts your hands back to the address or impact position.

The third part of your arm movement is a mirror image of the first or backswing move. This time it is your left arm that folds upward, with your right arm extending slightly as it is taken along for the ride. Your hands finish the drill in front of your left shoulder, with your left arm cocked at the elbow and the club shaft pointing up over your left shoulder.

To review this drill, in order to more clearly relay the instructional message, it requires you to employ an up-down-up movement as if you are drawing an imaginary V in front of your torso. On the first move up, your right arm folds upward. On the downward portion, your right arm again controls the motion by uncocking fully at the elbow. On the final segment, your left arm controls the movement by cocking upward, while your right arm takes a ride.

Practice this arm swing drill often. You must make each up or down movement aggressively. The movements of your arms as in this drill will be your primary source of power in the two-plane swing, so don't hold back. Cock and uncock each arm as fully as you can on each repetition.

The Arm Swing V Drill shows exactly how your arms would work if they were separated from your body turn. Of course, this movement must be blended with the body into the complete two-plane swing. Here's a good way to understand how the arms and the body work together. First, move your arms up into the backswing position as I've described, with your right elbow folding and the club shaft pointing up. Next, simply make a full body turn with your shoulders, torso, and hips. (If you are using the variation close to the wall, do not let the arms touch the wall). Where does this put you? Just cock your wrists and you are in an ideal top-of-the-backswing position for the two-plane swing. You have made a full turn so that your back is nearly facing the target. Your arms and hands are still in front of you—that is, in front of the right side of your chest. Further, because of the full turn of your shoulders, the club shaft (which as I said was pointing over your right shoulder) is now parallel to your target line at the top of the backswing.

That's all that a two-plane backswing is: An upward cocking of the arms plus a turn of the body, done with precise timing. Practice these two moves separately a dozen or so times. When you feel comfortable with them, gradually start making both moves at the same time. I recommend you practice in slow motion at first, then very gradually increase the speed to that of a smooth, controlled backswing, feeling the timing of moving your arms up and turning in unison.

You can and should do exactly the same swing to build your downswing and follow-through. For the downswing, uncock your right arm and swing your left arm down fully, bringing your hands down in front of your body. I refer to the downward move of the arms and the club as *separation*. When you uncock your right arm and swing your left arm down, you are separating both your forearms and the club away from your body. It is very important in the two-plane swing that you make a pure separation to drive the club back down to the ball. There must be no dipping whatsoever of the right shoulder in an effort to help the club back down. As discussed earlier in the Anti-Tilt Drill, dipping the shoulder throws the entire swing off plane and in the wrong direction. It also reduces the power you can achieve with a full separation of your arms.

You have now driven the club down to the base of the V (into the impact zone). Next, cock the club aggressively up with your left arm for the follow-through motion, with your right hand and arm extending so that your hands finish in front of your left shoulder.

Once you have done enough repetitions so that you feel sure of both the down and up arm movements of the downswing and follow-through, you can again begin blending these movements with the body turn for the downswing and follow-through. (Once again, if you are using the variation close to the wall, do not let the arms hit the wall in the backswing, downswing, or follow-through).

As you begin making your arm movements in unison with your downswing body turn, you may find that you need to work on timing your arm and body movements in the downswing a little longer than you did for the backswing. The reason is that on the downswing, you are timing two movements of the arms (downward separation, then back up) with the single sweeping movement of the body turn. At any rate, if at any point you feel uncomfortable with the movements either on the backswing, the downswing, or both, always go back and practice the arm and body movements separately. You will gradually start to feel the entire movement come together.

Ball-Flight Correction: The Arm Swing V Drill specifically trains you to keep your arms in front of your body throughout the swing. This drill is especially helpful to golfers who swing their arms and the club too far around and behind them on the backswing or lack the timing and coordination to swing their arms and turn their body in unison. When a player gets the club too far behind or he is out of timing while attempting to execute the two-plane swing, both pulled and pushed shots are a frequent result. Also, shots hit in the heel—even shanked—will occur much too frequently. The two-plane swinger who learns to keep the arms and the club in front of his body will find it easier to deliver the clubhead square to the back of the ball for straighter and more solid shots.

Two-Plane Release/Rotation Drill

Purpose: To show the two-plane swinger how and when to release and rotate the forearms and hands through the impact zone in order to return the clubface square to the ball at impact.

Procedure: One of the key differences between the one-plane and two-plane swing occurs in the area of the release through impact. In a one-plane release, the specific movement through impact is done on an in-to-in arc. There is only the required rotation of the left forearm during the downswing and into impact that is sufficient to bring the club square to the arc and keep it square to the arc (plane) during impact. However, in the two-plane swing, there must be a perfectly timed specific and active release through impact in which the golfer's right or rear forearm turns in a counterclockwise manner over the left or lead arm. The movement, by definition, must work the clubface from open prior to impact to square at impact and then closed again after impact. This is tremendously different from the one-plane player's action through the hitting zone (as well as being more complex). Among PGA Tour players, 2004 Masters champion Phil Mickelson provides a great example of a full forearm release through impact. If you watch Phil during a tournament, particularly when he is hitting a driver, you'll notice how aggressively he rotates his left forearm (which, being a left-handed player, is his rear forearm) over his right forearm in a clockwise manner.

I would like to interject a point here about why this conscious forearm rotation is necessary for the two-plane golfer. The main reason is that the two-plane swing is more upright and therefore on less of a circular arc. In the one-plane swing, the aggressive hip and shoulder turn hurls the arms, hands, and club around with it, so that the clubface, once the rotating left arm has returned it square to the plane or arc, moves from open to closed relative to the target by simply moving on the arc. The right arm begins its release just before impact but does not fully roll over until just past midway in the follow-through. However, as you know, the shoulders do not dominate in the two-plane swing and the arms do not travel around on as great an arc. Therefore, the arms and hands must work to square up the clubface at impact by rolling over far more and complete the roll-over far sooner than in the one-plane swing.

The focus of this drill is on the rotation of your forearms and the movement of the clubhead from the point at which the clubhead is at hip height in the downswing to when it is at hip height beyond impact. Take a middle iron and assume your address position. Next, bring the club back to a point where the club shaft is parallel to the ground just below hip height. The toe of the club must be pointing straight up. From here, slowly bring the club down while you gradually rotate your right or rear forearm in a counterclockwise manner (assuming you are a right-handed golfer). I recommend that when you begin this drill you stop when the club is at the point where it would strike the ball. Check to see if the leading edge of the clubface appears to be square to your target line. If it is open (pointing to the right) it means you have not rotated your right forearm enough. If the leading edge is closed (pointing left of target) it means you have rotated the right forearm too much. In my teaching experience, I would say that the vast majority of amateurs have too little forearm rotation, which contributes to an open clubface at impact and a slice-shot.

Keep working the club down in slow motion from just below hip height to impact, always checking to make sure your clubface returns to square. Once you have the feel of the rotation needed to return to square at impact, go back to your original position with the club shaft just below hip height behind you and the toe of the club pointing up. Now work your forearms and the club down and through the impact zone. But this time continue on up until the club is parallel to the ground and just below hip height beyond impact. Look carefully at the toe of the club. Is it pointing straight up? If you have continued to rotate your right forearm correctly over your left, the toe should point just slightly left of straight up. If the toe is pointing up or at an angle to your right as you face the target, that's a sure sign that you have not rotated the forearms completely, and thus the clubface is left open in relation to your swing path. If the toe of the clubface at this point is overly rotated so it is well left of toe-up (slightly left of toe-up is square), it is a sign of too much rotation or late rotation with too much happening after impact.

The drill in summary: Work the club between the two positions described so that it finishes correctly on either side of you. I recommend you do this drill as many times as you can, albeit it at a slow pace. Once you get to where you can consistently move the club from toe-up to square (slightly left of toe-up) through the impact zone, you can feel very confident that you will square up the clubface at impact during actual play.

A word of warning here: You may think that the Two-Plane Release/Rotation Drill is quite easy to master. You are right. But keep in mind that this conscious release is but one of three movements that must be well timed in order for you to develop an effective downswing. What I'm referring to, specifically, is timing your release with both the movement of the body in the two-plane downswing and with the down-and-up movement of the arms that we just discussed in the Arm Swing V Drill. This certainly can be done, of course, as so many great two-plane players have proven. However, I feel compelled to point out that while

Photos 5.20–5.22 **When practicing the Two-Plane Release/Rotation Drill, swing the club from toe-up position (left) to the toe-slightly-over position (center), making sure that you first rotate your right forearm correctly in order to arrive at impact with the clubface square (right).**

all these drills are very valuable, you will consistently need to work on your timing if you adopt the two-plane swing. That is the main reason I prefer that golfers use the one-plane swing if they are physically capable of doing so.

After you have practiced your two-plane release without a ball, it's a great exercise to practice short shots with this drill in mind. Take a nine-iron or a pitching wedge and make toe-up to toe-slightly-over swings, concentrating on employing a smooth but complete rotation of right forearm over left. Hit these shots toward a specific target 30 to 40 yards away. If you've assimilated this drill correctly, you should be able to keep the ball very much on target.

Ball-Flight Correction: The Two-Plane Release/Rotation Drill is especially helpful to anyone who either tends to hook the ball left or hits a slice. Working on it trains you to return the clubface square at impact through the correct amount of rotation of the wrists and forearms. So, with regular practice, your shots will soon start finding the target.

Index